# THE GARDEN OF
# GOD

D1571734

# BENEDICT XVI

## THE GARDEN OF

# GOD

## TOWARD A HUMAN ECOLOGY

*Edited by*
*Maria Milvia Morciano*

*With a foreword by*
*Archbishop Jean-Louis Bruguès, OP*

THE CATHOLIC UNIVERSITY OF AMERICA PRESS

WASHINGTON, D.C.

Originally published in Italian as *Per Una Ecologia dell'Uomo* by
the Libreria Editrice Vaticana, © 2012

Copyright © 2014
The Catholic University of America Press
The paper used in this publication meets the minimum requirements of
American National Standards for Information Science—Permanence
of Paper for Printed Library Materials, ANSI z39.48-1984.

∞

Library of Congress Cataloging-in-Publication Data
Benedict XVI, Pope, 1927–
[Per una ecologia dell'uomo. English]
The garden of God : toward a human ecology / Benedict XVI ; edited by
Maria Milvia Morciano ; with a foreword by Archbishop Jean-Louis Bruguès,
OP.
pages cm
Includes bibliographical references and index.
ISBN 978-0-8132-2579-1 (pbk. : alk. paper)
1. Human ecology—Religious aspects—Catholic Church.
2. Environmental justice—Religious aspects—Christianity.
3. Climatic changes.   4. Environmentalism—Religious aspects—
Catholic Church.   I. Morciano, Maria Milvia,
editor of compilation.   II. Title.
BX1795.H82B4513 2014
261.8'8—dc23      2013042122

# CONTENTS

CONTENTS

vi

## PART 3. HUNGER, POVERTY, AND THE EARTH'S RESOURCES

# FOREWORD

## *The Urgency of a Human Ecology*

In recent years, photovoltaic panels have been installed on the roof of the principal auditorium of the Vatican to produce electricity from the Roman sun. Its dining rooms now benefit from a solar cooling system. To compensate for its carbon dioxide emissions, the Vatican has begun to cultivate a several-hundred-acre climatic forest in Bükk (Hungary), thereby becoming the first climatically neutral country. Although it is true that the Vatican is the smallest country in the world, it is also true that in matters of ecology one cannot give advice to others if one does not start by applying that advice to oneself. In this field, witness has a greater value than discourse.

Nevertheless, discourse and documents are necessary: "The existence of such catastrophes challenges us," said Benedict XVI on June 9, 2011, while meeting with some new ambassadors. "Man comes first and it is necessary to remember this. Man, to whom God has entrusted the care of nature, cannot be dominated by technology and become an object of it. Such consciousness must bring all countries together to reflect on the near future of the planet, considering their responsibilities toward our lives and toward technology. Human ecology is an imperative

Translated by Marta Brown.

necessity. Adopting a way of life that is respectful of the environment in every circumstance and sustaining the research on and the utilization of adequate energies that safeguard the patrimony of creation and do not harm man, should be political and economic priorities. In this sense it becomes necessary to completely rethink our approach toward nature; nature is not only a resourceful or entertaining place. It is the place where man is born, his 'home.'"

I think that behind the widely accepted figure of the great intellectual we can distinguish another interesting figure; some people have called Benedict XVI "the green pope." Is this really true? The pontiffs have been discussing ecology for a long time: encyclicals, messages, and talks often confront the problem of human responsibility toward nature and the climate, yet everything happens as if a screen made their words inaudible. Why? There are structural causes for this lack: the Catholic parameters—long duration, patience, maturation, rootedness—are different from those of Western societies—instantaneity, the ephemeral, the anxiety of progress at any cost.

There is a second, more frightening difficulty. It takes on the form of an argument that is often repeated and presented as a reprimand: Christianity would have provided the ideological matrix of a certain modernity, which, considering nature as an ethically mute mine with inexhaustible resources, has conceived of progress as an almost infinite growth and development. This argument contains a measure of truth. There was in fact a current of thought, presented as the modern version of Christianity, which played this role. According to it, man would be at the center of the universe, which he would have to subordinate with the genius of his science and technology. This vision, which begins in the seventeenth century, is founded on the philosophy and the mechanistic conception of Descartes and develops into the so-called liberal theology. The latter, often of Protestant origin, presents Christianity as a religion which is radically different from all other religions.

Traditional pagan religions proposed a close and harmonious relationship between man and nature, which they believed to be inhabited by superior forms. They offered an ideal of life in the form of ancestral wisdom. According to this succinctly described current of thought, Christianity is essentially a historical religion, because God intervened in the history of man. Therefore it is necessary to look at history and not at nature to find the sense of human existence, to the future and not to our ancestors, at prophecy and not at wisdom.

This current of thought has played a predominant role since the end of the nineteenth century and for two-thirds of the last century. However, it is subject to the following reprimand: this Christianity did not preoccupy itself with nature nor with the elements connected to it.

Is it necessary to remember that Christianity is manifold? Other Christian traditions have emphasized the perception of nature as benevolent, a fountain of teaching entrusted to the respectful management of man. "If I look at your sky, the work of your hands, the moon and the stars that you set in place, what is man that you should remember him?" (Ps 8:4). De facto, since the origins of Christianity, there have been authors, and not unimportant ones, who have advocated for a harmonious relationship between man and creation. Origen believed that there was a resemblance between all creatures, obviously different from that of the human creature with the Creator. In the fourth century, Basil of Caesarea affirmed that "the world is the school of rational souls and the place in which one educates oneself in the knowledge of God, because He offers to the soul, through visible and sensory things, a guide to the penetrating knowledge of invisible realities" (*Homilies on the Hexaemeron* I, 6).

Maybe we are more attuned with the poetic figure of St. Francis of Assisi, who preached to all the creatures "with a great interior and exterior joy, as if they were capable of feeling, of intelligence, and of speaking" (testimony of brother Leone). This poetic mood will continue into the present time and is particularly strong in poets like Péguy.

Benedict XVI outlines a very clear choice between these two Christian visions. "If we want to understand Christianity again," Cardinal Ratzinger wrote, "and live it in all its depth, we have to peremptorily rediscover the cosmic dimension of revelation" (*Introduction to the Spirit of the Liturgy*). Thus, he breaks off from the first current of thought, which had exercised a more determined influence in Germany than in other places, and sides with what I would call the Franciscan line.

Joseph Ratzinger was the closest collaborator of Pope John Paul II, who greatly revered the figure of St. Francis of Assisi because his message invited one to break with violence and possessiveness, to change one's vision of nature, to feel for it a vital familiarity, and to decipher the world as a divine word. In the course of his pontificate, Pope John Paul II indicated the economic system that plunders the planet. The encyclical *Sollicitudo Rei Socialis* (1987) is in substance the critical face, or better, the combative face of Christian ecology. The biosphere is a whole: "One cannot impudently use the various categories of living or inanimate beings in any way one wants, according to his or her economic needs." Natural resources are limited: "Using them with absolute dominion as if they were inexhaustible puts their availability in serious danger" for the future generations. A certain type of development threatens the quality of life: "The contamination of the environment is more and more frequently a direct or indirect result of Industrialization."

Pope John Paul II, in his message for the World Day of Peace in 1990, which earned him the title "green khmer" from the neoconservatives, formulates what can be defined as the decalogue of ecology according to Christianity. He who would later become Benedict XVI played a large part in drawing it up. We will now cite a few of its ideas. The human journey toward the biosphere must choose a path of sobriety (n. 3). Every economic power which destroys the "delicate ecological balances" is fatal (n. 4). We must adopt a precautionary principle, especially in regard to genetically modified organisms (n. 6). Every country has the duty to "prevent the deterioration of the atmosphere and of the biosphere" in its own territory (n. 8). The Church, like the radical ecologists, sees a tie between the environment, the social, the economy, and politics, but adds to it the ethical dimension, in which she perceives a key for changing reality. It is not enough just to recognize these ties; it is also necessary to analyze them and justify them. This will be the task of Benedict XVI, who will earn the title of "green pope."

Benedict XVI has spoken about ecology more than any of his predecessors. On the vigil of Pentecost in 2006, he invited Catholics all over the world to protect creation against egotistical exploitation: "Those very people who, as Christians, believe in the Creator Spirit become aware of the fact that we cannot use and abuse the world and matter merely as material for our actions and desires; that we must consider creation a gift that has not been given to us to be destroyed, but to become God's garden, hence, a garden for men and women." The image of the garden, characteristic of the Franciscan sensibility, reappears here.

These ideas are developed and expounded upon in three fundamental texts that allow us to "think ecology": the message given to the world on the occasion of the World Day of Peace on January 1, 2010, which was released before the full conference of Copenhagen; the encyclical *Caritas in Veritate,* signed in June of 2009; and the talk mentioned above from June 3, 2006.

There are five principles which emerge from these texts.

The first principle: *it is man that comes first.* Man is, if I am permitted to say it, the alpha and the omega of development, the agent and the recipient. Good ecological choices respect the dignity of the person and his or her fundamental rights. This view is opposed to a utilitarian conception in which the ends justify the means. As Kant wrote, the human person should never be treated as a means but always as an end. The centrality of the human person avoids putting everything that exists on the same level of equality, to the point of talking about the rights of animals and plants or even those of matter. It is an absolutely sectarian risk, which has the goal of pushing people to forget that only man was created in the image of God. Such a statement does not take away the fact that man has duties toward the inferior creatures that have been entrusted to his care.

The second principle: *man cannot be dominated by technology.* Ecology is first of all an ethical question. Of course, it must be based on technological means, but technology cannot respond to all the challenges thrown toward the "safeguard of the heritage of creation." The risk of a technological civilization is that it will allow people to believe that technology will resolve any problem. In reality, ethics are necessary if we do not want man to become a slave of technology.

The third principle: *nature is inhabited.* In substance, ecology should not be founded on a relationship of power and of domination, as in the cases of extreme exploitation, but on an alliance, on a harmonious relationship between the human being and development (*Caritas in Veritate* n. 50). Here, with the already spoken of Franciscan tone, we find what we can call the professing dimension of Christian ecology. Nature is not the result of chance or necessity; for the believer it is "the expression of a loving and truthful design" (ibid., n. 48). A similar conception allows us to discard a mechanistic and utilitarian view. "Nature is at our disposal not as 'a random pile of garbage' (Heraclitus), but as a gift from the Creator who designed its intrinsic order so that man might derive from it the principle necessary to 'take care of it and cultivate it' (Genesis 2:15)." It is to man that God has entrusted the proper care of nature. Man, through his reason and his wisdom, and so through a cultural effort, can become capable of "reading" nature and of learning lessons from it to conduct his existence. The Christian perspective could not correspond more to the neopagan or pantheistic views which are in style in our day and which make nature a superior and in some way divine entity, greater than man.

The fourth principle: *in reality, the human race is a family.* The relations between the members of a family are marked by a double solidarity, that which unites the members who are present in a brotherly way (sharing), and that which unites generations (prevision). The same should happen at the global level. This presupposes that the men of our age care for the future generations (cf. *Caritas in Veritate* n. 48), and that the hoarding of the nonrenewable energy resources on the part of some (countries or enterprises) leave space for a sharing with the poorer countries. The difficulty of the latter challenge is evident: are the technologically advanced societies willing to diminish their energy consumption? How can we conceive a redistribution of energy resources at the global level?

The fifth principle: it therefore becomes necessary to *change mentality.* Things cannot continue in this way: resources will be exhausted, creation will degrade. It is necessary and even urgent to change our way of life. "The change of mentality in this area, better the obligations that this entails, must allow us to quickly find an art of living together that respects the alliance between man and nature, without which the human family risks disappearing."

Such a change must bring us to adopt new styles of life marked by sobriety (the consumerist mentality will not like this principle). Ecology does not only reveal the relationship between man and the environment, but also man's relationship with himself: "Duties toward the environment derive from those toward the person considered in itself and in relation to others" (Message for the World Day of Peace 2010). The way in which man refers to his consumption, his hygiene, his sexuality, his conception of otherness, culture, his role in the cities, allows him to outline a true human ecology, namely a new art of living.

Benedict XVI is prophetic when he declares, "The world is in need of profound cultural renewal, a world that needs to re-discover fundamental values on which to build a better future. The current crisis obliges us to re-plan our journey, to set ourselves new rules and to discover new forms of commitment, to build on positive experiences and to reject negative ones. The crisis thus becomes *an opportunity for discernment, in which to shape a new vision for the future* (ibid.). Will his appeals for a more sober way of life and more controlled consumption patterns, which question the dogma of popular consumerism, be listened to? One does not ask prophets to be popular; the real ones never are. It is to be expected that they will bother. After the failure of Durban, this "green pope" does not lose the occasion to do it.

Since the beginning of the eighties when the themes of ecology and sustainable development began to make their debut in public debate, their importance has been steadily increasing, to the point of becoming major political claims. These themes, which for a long time were considered "Western," that is, for rich countries, have now begun to appear in the development programs of the other countries. One cannot but be happy. It will not be surprising to see that the younger generations are more sensitive than the previous ones: after all, it is about their future. In this field, like in many others, the Church has done more than just accompany the movement; it has often preceded it. The following pages are the proof of this fact.

ARCHBISHOP JEAN-LOUIS BRUGUÈS
*Secretary of the Congregation for Catholic Education*

PART 1

CREATION AND
NATURE

## In Contact with Nature,
## Individuals Rediscover That They Are
## Creatures "Capable of God"

From Angelus, Les Combes (Aosta Valley), July 17, 2005

In the world in which we live, the need to be physically and mentally replenished has become as it were essential, especially to those who dwell in cities where the often frenzied pace of life leaves little room for silence, reflection, and relaxing contact with nature. Moreover, holidays are days on which we can give even more time to prayer, reading, and meditation on the profound meaning of life in the peaceful context of our own family and loved ones. The vacation period affords unique opportunities for reflection as we face the stirring views of nature, a marvelous "book" within the reach of everyone, adults or children. In contact with nature, individuals rediscover their proper dimension, they recognize that they are creatures but at the same time unique, "capable of God" since they are inwardly open to the Infinite. Driven by the heartfelt need for meaning that urges them onward, they perceive the mark of goodness and divine Providence in the world that surrounds them and open themselves almost spontaneously to praise and prayer.

## Creation Is a Gift So That It Might Become the Garden of God and Hence a Garden for Men and Women

Let us ask ourselves now, at this Pentecost Vigil, who or what is the Holy Spirit? How can we recognize him? How do we go to him and how does he come to us? What does he do?

The Church's great Pentecostal hymn with which we began Vespers, *"Veni, Creator Spiritus* ... Come, Holy Spirit," gives us a first answer. Here the hymn refers to the first verses of the Bible that describe the creation of the universe with recourse to images.

The Bible says first of all that the Spirit of God was moving over the chaos, over the waters of the abyss.

The world in which we live is the work of the Creator Spirit. Pentecost is not only the origin of the Church and thus in a special way her feast; Pentecost is also a feast of creation. The world does not exist by itself; it is brought into being by the creative Spirit of God, by the creative Word of God.

For this reason Pentecost also mirrors God's wisdom. In its breadth and in the omni-comprehensive logic of its laws, God's wisdom permits us to glimpse something of his Creator Spirit. It elicits reverential awe.

Those very people who, as Christians, believe in the Creator Spirit become aware of the fact that we cannot use and abuse

4

the world and matter merely as material for our actions and desires; that we must consider creation a gift that has not been given to us to be destroyed, but to become God's garden, hence, a garden for men and women.

In the face of the many forms of abuse of the earth that we see today, let us listen, as it were, to the groaning of creation of which St. Paul speaks (Rom 8:22); let us begin by understanding the Apostle's words, that creation waits with impatience for the revelation that we are children of God, to be set free from bondage and obtain his splendor.

Dear friends, we want to be these children of God for whom creation is waiting, and we can become them because the Lord has made us such in Baptism. Yes, creation and history—they are waiting for us, for men and women who are truly children of God and behave as such.

If we look at history, we see that creation prospered around monasteries, just as with the reawakening of God's Spirit in human hearts the brightness of the Creator Spirit has also been restored to the earth—a splendor that has been clouded and at times even extinguished by the barbarity of the human mania for power.

Moreover, the same thing happened once again around Francis of Assisi—it has happened everywhere as God's Spirit penetrates souls, this Spirit whom our hymn describes as light, love, and strength.

Thus, we have discovered an initial answer to the question as to what the Holy Spirit is, what he does, and how we can recognize him. He comes to meet us through creation and its beauty.

However, in the course of human history, a thick layer of

dirt has covered God's good creation, which makes it difficult if not impossible to perceive in it the Creator's reflection, although the knowledge of the Creator's existence is reawakened within us ever anew, as it were, spontaneously, at the sight of a sunset over the sea, on an excursion to the mountains or before a flower that has just bloomed.

But the Creator Spirit comes to our aid. He has entered history and speaks to us in a new way. In Jesus Christ, God himself was made man and allowed us, so to speak, to cast a glance at the intimacy of God himself.

And there we see something totally unexpected: in God, an "I" and a "You" exist. The mysterious God is not infinite loneliness, he is an event of love. If by gazing at creation we think we can glimpse the Creator Spirit, God himself, rather like creative mathematics, like a force that shapes the laws of the world and their order, but then, even, also like beauty—now we come to realize: the Creator Spirit has a heart. He is Love.

The Son who speaks to the Father exists and they are both one in the Spirit, who constitutes, so to speak, the atmosphere of giving and loving which makes them one God. This unity of love which is God, is a unity far more sublime than the unity of a last indivisible particle could be. The Triune God himself is the one and only God.

## Creation, with All of Its Gifts, Aspires Above and Beyond Itself

From Homily for the Holy Mass and
Eucharistic Procession on the Solemnity
of the Sacred Body and Blood of Christ,
Saint John Lateran, June 15, 2006

On the eve of his Passion, during the Passover meal, the Lord took the bread in his hands—as we heard a short time ago in the Gospel passage—and, having blessed it, he broke it and gave it to his disciples, saying: "Take this, this is my body." He then took the chalice, gave thanks, and passed it to them and they all drank from it. He said: "This is my blood, the blood of the covenant, to be poured out on behalf of many" (Mk 14:22–24).

The entire history of God with humanity is recapitulated in these words. The past alone is not only referred to and interpreted, but the future is anticipated—the coming of the Kingdom of God into the world. What Jesus says are not simply words. What he says is an event, the central event of the history of the world and of our personal lives.

These words are inexhaustible. In this hour, I would like to meditate with you on just one aspect. Jesus, as a sign of his presence, chose bread and wine. With each one of the two signs he gives himself completely, not only in part. The Risen One is not divided. He is a person who, through signs, comes near to us and unites himself to us.

Each sign however, represents in its own way a particular aspect of his mystery and through its respective manifestation, wishes to speak to us so that we learn to understand the mystery of Jesus Christ a little better.

During the procession and in adoration we look at the consecrated Host, the most simple type of bread and nourishment, made only of a little flour and water. In this way, it appears as the food of the poor, those to whom the Lord made himself closest in the first place.

The prayer with which the Church, during the liturgy of the Mass, consigns this bread to the Lord, qualifies it as fruit of the earth and the work of humans.

It involves human labor, the daily work of those who till the soil, sow and harvest [the wheat], and, finally, prepare the bread. However, bread is not purely and simply what we produce, something made by us; it is fruit of the earth and therefore is also gift.

We cannot take credit for the fact that the earth produces fruit; the Creator alone could have made it fertile. And now we too can expand a little on this prayer of the Church, saying: the bread is fruit of heaven and earth together. It implies the synergy of the forces of earth and the gifts from above, that is, of the sun and the rain. And water too, which we need to prepare the bread, cannot be produced by us.

In a period in which desertification is spoken of and where we hear time and again the warning that man and beast risk dying of thirst in these waterless regions—in such a period we realize once again how great is the gift of water and of how we are unable to produce it ourselves.

And so, looking closely at this little piece of white Host, this bread of the poor, appears to us as a synthesis of creation. Heaven and earth, too, like the activity and spirit of man, cooperate.

The synergy of the forces that make the mystery of life and the existence of man possible on our poor planet come to meet us in all of their majestic grandeur.

In this way we begin to understand why the Lord chooses this piece of bread to represent him. Creation, with all of its gifts, aspires above and beyond itself to something even greater. Over and above the synthesis of its own forces, above and beyond the synthesis also of nature and of spirit that, in some way, we detect in the piece of bread, creation is projected toward divinization, toward the holy wedding feast, toward unification with the Creator himself.

And still, we have not yet explained in depth the message of this sign of bread. The Lord mentioned its deepest mystery on Palm Sunday, when some Greeks asked to see him. In his answer to this question is the phrase: "Truly, truly, I say to you, unless a grain of wheat falls into the earth and dies, it remains alone; but if it dies, it bears much fruit" (Jn 12:24).

The mystery of the Passion is hidden in the bread made of ground grain. Flour, the ground wheat, presupposes the death and resurrection of the grain. In being ground and baked, it carries in itself once again the same mystery of the Passion. Only through death does resurrection arrive, as does the fruit and new life.

Mediterranean culture, in the centuries before Christ, had a profound intuition of this mystery. Based on the experience of this death and rising they created myths of divinity which, dying and rising, gave new life. To them, the cycle of nature seemed like a divine promise in the midst of the darkness of suffering and death that we are faced with.

In these myths, the soul of the human person, in a certain way, reached out toward that God made man, who, humiliated unto death on a cross, in this way opened the door of life to all of us. In bread and its making, man has understood it as a waiting period of nature, like a promise of nature that this would come to exist: the God that dies and in this way brings us to life. What was awaited in myths and that in the very grain of wheat is hidden like a sign of the hope of creation—this truly came about in Christ. Through his gratuitous suffering and death, he became bread for all of us, and with this living and certain hope. He accompanies us in all of our sufferings until death. The paths that he travels with us and through which he leads us to life are pathways of hope.

## The Amazon River, a Fountain of Life

From Letter to His Holiness Bartholomew I,
Ecumenical Patriarch, on the Occasion of the
Sixth Symposium on Religion, Science, and the
Environment Focusing on the Amazon River,
July 6, 2006

Since I am unable to be present in person at the new and important meeting for the safeguard of creation, which you have organized with the Sixth Symposium on "Religion, Science, and the Environment," dedicated to the Amazon River, I entrust the task of bringing you my cordial greeting to Cardinal Roger Etchegaray.

I am grateful to you, Your Holiness, for having arranged that the preparation of the symposium take place in close collaboration with the Catholic Bishops' Conference of Brazil.

In fact, Cardinal Geraldo Majella Agnelo, Archbishop of São Salvador da Bahia, will be taking part and will not fail to express my gratitude to you for your support of the work of the Brazilian Episcopate in Amazonia and its action on behalf of the environment, whose deterioration has profound and serious repercussions on the population.

The joint effort to create awareness on the part of Christians of every denomination, in order to show "the intrinsic connection between development, human need and the stewardship of creation," is truly proving more important than ever.[1]

In this context, I remember Pope John Paul II of venerable memory supporting the Fourth Symposium on the Adriatic Sea, and I also remember the Common Declaration that he signed with you, Venerable Brother.

The duty to emphasize an appropriate catechesis concerning creation, in order to recall the meaning and religious significance of protecting it, is closely connected with our duty as pastors and can have an important impact on the perception of the value of life itself as well as on the satisfactory solution of the consequent inevitable social problems.

I warmly hope, Your Holiness, that the Sixth Symposium dedicated to the Amazon River will once again attract the attention of peoples and governments to the problems, needs, and emergencies of a region so harshly tried and whose ecological balance is so threatened: in their majestic beauty, its rivers and forests speak to us of God and of his grandiose work for humanity.

1. *Directory for the Application of the Principles and Norms of Ecumenism,* 1993, n. 215.

This immense region, where waters are an incomparable source of harmony and riches, is presented as an open book whose pages reveal the mystery of life.

How is it possible not to feel, both as individuals and as communities, urged to acquire a responsible awareness that is expressed in consistent decisions to protect such an ecologically rich environment?

With this symposium, Your Holiness, you have wished to express—over and above any other consideration and there would be many of them—the Christian support for the peoples in the Amazon regions, a support, in short, that stems from contemplation of the eternal Word of God, the Author, Model, and End of all things.

As I express to you, Your Holiness, my deep appreciation of the intentions that inspire you, I would like to assure you of my support for the values inherent in the symposium. I see our common commitment as an example of that collaboration which Orthodox and Catholics must constantly seek, to respond to the call for a common witness.

This implies that all Christians seriously cultivate the mental openness that is dictated by love and rooted in faith. Thus, they will be able together to offer to the world a credible witness of their sense of responsibility for the safeguard of creation.

At the Sixth Symposium dedicated to the Amazon River, prominent figures and experts will be taking part who belong to the great monotheistic religions. Their presence is important.

There are practical objectives that are a matter of survival for man and can and must bring together all people of good will.

Reciprocal respect also passes through projects such as this event, because the topics that will be addressed are of common interest to all.

Common points must be found on which converge the commitments of each one to safeguard the habitat that the Creator has made available to the human being, in whom he has impressed his own image.

Your Holiness, I ask you to convey my most cordial good wishes to all who are taking part in the symposium and to assure them of my prayers that it will constitute an important step forward in the effort, so widely shared, to safeguard this world that God created with wisdom and love (cf. Ps 104 [103]).

I exchange a fraternal embrace with you, Your Holiness, in the Name of the One Lord.

## The "Ecology of Peace"

From Message for the Celebration of the
Fortieth World Day of Peace,
January 1, 2007

8. In his encyclical letter *Centesimus Annus,* Pope John Paul II wrote: "Not only has God given the earth to man, who must use it with respect for the original good purpose for which it was given to him, but man too is God's gift to man. He must therefore respect the natural and moral structure with which he has been endowed."[2] By responding to this charge, entrusted to them by the Creator, men and women can join in bringing about a world of peace. Alongside the ecology of nature, there

2. Cf. *Catechism of the Catholic Church* (1993), n. 357.

exists what can be called a "human" ecology, which in turn demands a "social" ecology. All this means that humanity, if it truly desires peace, must be increasingly conscious of the links between natural ecology, or respect for nature, and human ecology. Experience shows that *disregard for the environment always harms human coexistence,* and vice versa. It becomes more and more evident that there is an inseparable link between peace with creation and peace among men. Both of these presuppose peace with God. The poem-prayer of St. Francis, known as "the Canticle of Brother Sun," is a wonderful and ever timely example of this multifaceted ecology of peace.

9. The close connection between these two ecologies can be understood from the increasingly serious problem of *energy supplies.* In recent years, new nations have entered enthusiastically into industrial production, thereby increasing their energy needs. This has led to an unprecedented race for available resources. Meanwhile, some parts of the planet remain backward and development is effectively blocked, partly because of the rise in energy prices. What will happen to those peoples? What kind of development or non-development will be imposed on them by the scarcity of energy supplies? What injustices and conflicts will be provoked by the race for energy sources? And what will be the reaction of those who are excluded from this race? These are questions that show how respect for nature is closely linked to the need to establish, between individuals and between nations, relationships that are attentive to the dignity of the person and capable of satisfying his or her authentic needs. The destruction of the environment, its improper or selfish use, and the violent hoarding of the earth's resources cause

grievances, conflicts, and wars, precisely because they are the consequences of an inhumane concept of development. Indeed, if development were limited to the technical-economic aspect, obscuring the moral-religious dimension, it would not be an integral human development, but a one-sided distortion which would end up by unleashing man's destructive capacities.

## REDUCTIVE VISIONS OF MAN

10. Thus there is an urgent need, even within the framework of current international difficulties and tensions, for a commitment to *a human ecology that can favor the growth of the "tree of peace."* For this to happen, we must be guided by a vision of the person untainted by ideological and cultural prejudices or by political and economic interests which can instill hatred and violence. It is understandable that visions of man will vary from culture to culture. Yet what cannot be admitted is the cultivation of *anthropological conceptions* that contain the seeds of hostility and violence. Equally unacceptable are *conceptions of God* that would encourage intolerance and recourse to violence against others. This is a point which must be clearly reaffirmed: war *in God's name* is never acceptable! When a certain notion of God is at the origin of criminal acts, it is a sign that that notion has already become an ideology.

11. Today, however, peace is not only threatened by the conflict between reductive visions of man, in other words, between ideologies. It is also threatened by *indifference as to what constitutes man's true nature.* Many of our contemporaries actually deny the existence of a specific human nature and thus open the door to the most extravagant interpretations of what essential-

ly constitutes a human being. Here too clarity is necessary: a "weak" vision of the person, which would leave room for every conception, even the most bizarre, only apparently favors peace. In reality, it hinders authentic dialogue and opens the way to authoritarian impositions, ultimately leaving the person defenseless and, as a result, easy prey to oppression and violence.

## HUMAN RIGHTS AND INTERNATIONAL ORGANIZATIONS

12. A true and stable peace presupposes respect for human rights. Yet if these rights are grounded on a weak conception of the person, how can they fail to be themselves weakened? Here we can see how profoundly insufficient is *a relativistic conception of the person* when it comes to justifying and defending his rights. The difficulty in this case is clear: rights are proposed as absolute, yet the foundation on which they are supposed to rest is merely relative. Can we wonder that, faced with the "inconvenient" demands posed by one right or another, someone will come along to question it or determine that it should be set aside? Only if they are grounded in the objective requirements of the nature bestowed on man by the Creator, can the rights attributed to him be affirmed without fear of contradiction. It goes without saying, moreover, that human rights imply corresponding duties. In this regard, Mahatma Gandhi said wisely: "The Ganges of rights flows from the Himalaya of duties." Clarity over these basic presuppositions is needed if human rights, nowadays constantly under attack, are to be adequately defended. Without such clarity, the expression "human rights" will end up being predicated of quite different subjects: in some cas-

es, the human person marked by permanent dignity and rights that are valid always, everywhere, and for everyone, in other cases a person with changing dignity and constantly negotiable rights, with regard to content, time, and place.

15. Another disturbing issue is the desire recently shown by some states to *acquire nuclear weapons.* This has heightened even more the widespread climate of uncertainty and fear of a possible atomic catastrophe. We are brought back in time to the profound anxieties of the "cold war" period. When it came to an end, there was hope that the atomic peril had been definitively overcome and that mankind could finally breathe a lasting sigh of relief. How timely, in this regard, is the warning of the Second Vatican Council that "every act of war directed to the indiscriminate destruction of whole cities or vast areas with their inhabitants is a crime against God and humanity, which merits firm and unequivocal condemnation."[3] Unfortunately, threatening clouds continue to gather on humanity's horizon. The way to ensure a future of peace for everyone is found not only in international accords for *the non-proliferation of nuclear weapons,* but also in the determined commitment to seek their reduction and definitive dismantling. May every attempt be made to arrive through negotiation at the attainment of these objectives! The fate of the whole human family is at stake!

---

3. Second Vatican Council, Pastoral Constitution *Gaudium et Spes* (December 7, 1965), n. 80.

## Man Has Received Creation So That
## He Might Implement God's Plan

From Address on the Occasion of the Visit of His Beatitude
Chrysostomos II, Archbishop of Nea Justiniana and All Cyprus,
to His Holiness Benedict XVI, June 16, 2007

1. We, Benedict XVI, Pope and Bishop of Rome, and Chrysostomos II, Archbishop of Nea Justiniana and All Cyprus, full of hope for the future of our Churches' relations, thank God with joy for this fraternal meeting in our common faith in the Risen Christ. This visit has enabled us to observe how these relations have increased, both at a local level and in the context of the theological dialogue between the Catholic Church and the Orthodox Church as a whole....

8. At the same time, these ethical considerations and a shared concern for human life prompt us to invite those nations which, with God's grace, have made significant progress in the areas of the economy and technology, not to forget their brothers and sisters who live in countries afflicted by poverty, hunger, and disease. We therefore ask the leaders of nations to encourage and promote an equitable distribution of the goods of the earth in a spirit of solidarity with the poor and with all those who are destitute in the world.

9. We also concurred in our anxiety about the risk of destroying the creation. Man received it so that he might implement God's plan. However, by setting himself up at the center of the universe, forgetting the Creator's mandate and shutting himself in a selfish search for his own well-being, the human be-

ing has managed the environment in which he lives by putting into practice decisions that threaten his own existence, whereas the environment requires the respect and protection of all who dwell in it.

## *The Arctic: Mirror of Life*

From Letter to the Ecumenical Patriarch of
Constantinople on the Occasion of the Seventh Symposium
of the Religion, Science, and the Environment Movement,
September 1, 2007

It gives me great joy to greet you and all those taking part in the Seventh Symposium of the Religion, Science, and the Environment movement, which this year turns its attention to the subject: "The Arctic: Mirror of Life." Your own dedication and personal commitment to the protection of the environment demonstrates the pressing need for science and religion to work together to safeguard the gifts of nature and to promote responsible stewardship. Through the presence of Cardinal Mc-Carrick I wish to reaffirm my fervent solidarity with the aims of the project and to assure you of my hope for a deepening global recognition of the vital relationship between the ecology of the human person and the ecology of nature.[4]

Preservation of the environment, promotion of sustainable development, and particular attention to climate change are matters of grave concern for the entire human family. No nation or business sector can ignore the ethical implications present in

4. Cf. Benedict XVI, Message for the 2007 World Day of Peace, n. 8, January 1, 2007.

all economic and social development. With increasing clarity scientific research demonstrates that the impact of human actions in any one place or region can have worldwide effects. The consequences of disregard for the environment cannot be limited to an immediate area or populace because they always harm human coexistence, and thus betray human dignity and violate the rights of citizens who desire to live in a safe environment.[5]

This year's symposium, dedicated again to the earth's water resources, takes you and various religious leaders, scientists, and other interested parties to the Ilulissat Icefjord on the west coast of Greenland. Gathered in the magnificent beauty of this unique glacial region and World Heritage site your hearts and minds turn readily to the wonders of God and in awe echo the words of the psalmist praising the name of the Lord who is "majestic in all the earth." Immersed in contemplation of the "work of his fingers" (Ps 8), the perils of spiritual alienation from creation become plainly evident. The relationship between individuals or communities and the environment ultimately stems from their relationship with God. When "man turns his back on the Creator's plan, he provokes a disorder which has inevitable repercussions on the rest of the created order."[6]

Your Holiness, the international and multidisciplinary nature of the symposium attests to the need to seek global solutions to the matters under consideration. I am encouraged by the growing recognition that the entire human community—children and adults, industry sectors, states and international bodies—must take seriously the responsibility that falls to each

5. Cf. ibid., nn. 8–9.
6. John Paul II, Message for the 1990 World Day of Peace, n. 5, January 1, 1990.

and every one of us. While it is true that industrializing countries are not morally free to repeat the past errors of others, by recklessly continuing to damage the environment,[7] it is also the case that highly industrialized countries must share "clean technologies" and ensure that their own markets do not sustain demand for goods whose very production contributes to the proliferation of pollution. Mutual interdependence between nations' economic and social activities demands international solidarity, cooperation, and ongoing educational efforts. It is these principles which the religion, science, and the environment movement courageously upholds.

With sentiments of deep appreciation, and mindful of our commitment to encourage and support all efforts made to protect God's works,[8] I pray that the Almighty will abundantly bless this year's symposium. May he accompany you and all those gathered with you, so that all creation may give praise to God!

## The Wonder of Creation and the Scars Which Mark the Surface of the Earth

From Address at the Welcoming Celebration by the
Young People, Apostolic Journey to Sydney (Australia) on the
Occasion of the Twenty-third World Youth Day,
Barangaroo, Sydney Harbor, July 17, 2008

For some of us, it might seem like we have come to the end of the world! For people of your age, however, any flight is an

7. Cf. ibid., n. 10.

8. Cf. Benedict XVI and Bartholomew I, Common Declaration, Apostolic Journey to Turkey, November 30, 2006.

exciting prospect. But for me, this one was somewhat daunting! Yet the views afforded of our planet from the air were truly wondrous. The sparkle of the Mediterranean, the grandeur of the North African desert, the lushness of Asia's forestation, the vastness of the Pacific Ocean, the horizon upon which the sun rose and set, and the majestic splendor of Australia's natural beauty which I have been able to enjoy these last couple of days; these all evoke a profound sense of awe. It is as though one catches glimpses of the Genesis creation story—light and darkness, the sun and the moon, the waters, the earth, and living creatures; all of which are "good" in God's eyes (cf. Gn 1:1–2:4). Immersed in such beauty, who could not echo the words of the psalmist in praise of the Creator: "how majestic is your name in all the earth?" (Ps 8:1).

And there is more—something hardly perceivable from the sky—men and women, made in nothing less than God's own image and likeness (cf. Gn 1:26). At the heart of the marvel of creation are you and I, the human family "crowned with glory and honor" (Ps 8:5). How astounding! With the psalmist we whisper: "what is man that you are mindful of him?" (Ps 8:4). And drawn into silence, into a spirit of thanksgiving, into the power of holiness, we ponder.

What do we discover? Perhaps reluctantly we come to acknowledge that there are also scars which mark the surface of our earth: erosion, deforestation, the squandering of the world's mineral and ocean resources in order to fuel an insatiable consumption. Some of you come from island nations whose very existence is threatened by rising water levels; others from nations suffering the effects of devastating drought. God's wondrous creation is sometimes experienced as almost hostile to its stewards, even something dangerous. How can what is "good" appear so threatening?

And there is more. What of man, the apex of God's creation? Every day we encounter the genius of human achievement. From advances in medical sciences and the wise application of technology, to the creativity reflected in the arts, the quality and enjoyment of people's lives in many ways are steadily rising. Among yourselves there is a readiness to take up the plentiful opportunities offered to you. Some of you excel in studies, sport, music, or dance and drama, others of you have a keen sense of social justice and ethics, and many of you take up service and voluntary work. All of us, young and old, have those moments when the innate goodness of the human person—perhaps glimpsed in the gesture of a little child or an adult's readiness to forgive—fills us with profound joy and gratitude.

Yet such moments do not last. So again, we ponder. And we discover that not only the natural but also the social environment—the habitat we fashion for ourselves—has its scars; wounds indicating that something is amiss. Here too, in our personal lives and in our communities, we can encounter a hostility, something dangerous; a poison which threatens to corrode what is good, reshape who we are, and distort the purpose for which we have been created. Examples abound, as you yourselves know. Among the more prevalent are alcohol and drug abuse, and the exaltation of violence and sexual degradation, often presented through television and the Internet as entertainment. I ask myself, could anyone standing face to face with people who actually do suffer violence and sexual exploitation "explain" that these tragedies, portrayed in virtual form, are considered merely "entertainment"?

There is also something sinister which stems from the fact that freedom and tolerance are so often separated from truth. This is fuelled by the notion, widely held today, that there are no absolute truths to guide our lives. Relativism, by indiscriminately giving value to practically everything, has made "experience" all-important. Yet, experiences, detached from any consideration of what is good or true, can lead, not to genuine freedom, but to moral or intellectual confusion, to a lowering of standards, to a loss of self-respect, and even to despair.

Dear friends, life is not governed by chance; it is not random. Your very existence has been willed by God, blessed and given a purpose (cf. Gn 1:28)! Life is not just a succession of events or experiences, helpful though many of them are. It is a search for the true, the good, and the beautiful. It is to this end that we make our choices; it is for this that we exercise our freedom; it is in this—in truth, in goodness, and in beauty—that we find happiness and joy. Do not be fooled by those who see you as just another consumer in a market of undifferentiated possibilities, where choice itself becomes the good, novelty usurps beauty, and subjective experience displaces truth.

Christ offers more! Indeed he offers everything! Only he who is the Truth can be the Way and hence also the Life. Thus the "way" which the Apostles brought to the ends of the earth is life in Christ. This is the life of the Church. And the entrance to this life, to the Christian way, is Baptism.

This evening I wish therefore to recall briefly something of our understanding of Baptism before tomorrow considering the

Holy Spirit. On the day of your Baptism, God drew you into his holiness (cf. 2 Pt 1:4). You were adopted as a son or daughter of the Father. You were incorporated into Christ. You were made a dwelling place of his Spirit (cf. 1 Cor 6:19). Indeed, toward the conclusion of your Baptism, the priest turned to your parents and those gathered and, calling you by your name, said: "You have become a new creation."[9]

Dear friends, in your homes, schools, and universities, in your places of work and recreation, remember that you are a new creation! As Christians you stand in this world knowing that God has a human face—Jesus Christ—the "way" who satisfies all human yearning, and the "life" to which we are called to bear witness, walking always in his light.[10]

The task of witness is not easy. There are many today who claim that God should be left on the sidelines, and that religion and faith, while fine for individuals, should either be excluded from the public forum altogether or included only in the pursuit of limited pragmatic goals. This secularist vision seeks to explain human life and shape society with little or no reference to the Creator. It presents itself as neutral, impartial, and inclusive of everyone. But in reality, like every ideology, secularism imposes a worldview. If God is irrelevant to public life, then society will be shaped in a godless image. When God is eclipsed, our ability to recognize the natural order, purpose, and the "good" begins to wane. What was ostensibly promoted as human ingenuity soon manifests itself as folly, greed, and selfish exploitation. And so we have become more and more aware of

9. Rite of Baptism, n. 99.
10. Cf. Rite of Baptism, n. 100.

our need for humility before the delicate complexity of God's world.

But what of our social environment? Are we equally alert to the signs of turning our back on the moral structure with which God has endowed humanity?[11] Do we recognize that the innate dignity of every individual rests on his or her deepest identity— as image of the Creator—and therefore that human rights are universal, based on the natural law, and not something dependent upon negotiation or patronage, let alone compromise? And so we are led to reflect on what place the poor and the elderly, immigrants and the voiceless, have in our societies. How can it be that domestic violence torments so many mothers and children? How can it be that the most wondrous and sacred human space—the womb—has become a place of unutterable violence?

My dear friends, God's creation is one and it is good. The concerns for non-violence, sustainable development, justice and peace, and care for our environment are of vital importance for humanity. They cannot, however, be understood apart from a profound reflection upon the innate dignity of every human life from conception to natural death: a dignity conferred by God himself and thus inviolable. Our world has grown weary of greed, exploitation, and division, of the tedium of false idols and piecemeal responses, and the pain of false promises. Our hearts and minds are yearning for a vision of life where love endures, where gifts are shared, where unity is built, where freedom finds meaning in truth, and where identity is found in respectful communion. This is the work of the Holy Spirit! This is the hope held

11. Cf. Benedict XVI, Message for the 2007 World Day of Peace, n. 8, January 1, 2007.

out by the Gospel of Jesus Christ. It is to bear witness to this reality that you were created anew at Baptism and strengthened through the gifts of the Spirit at Confirmation. Let this be the message that you bring from Sydney to the world!

## What Air Is for Biological Life, the Holy Spirit Is for Spiritual Life

From Homily for Eucharistic Celebration on the
Solemnity of Pentecost, May 31, 2009

Every time we celebrate the Eucharist we live in faith the mystery that is fulfilled on the altar, that is, we take part in the supreme act of love that Christ accomplished with his death and Resurrection. The one and only center of the liturgy and Christian life itself the Paschal Mystery acquires in the various solemnities and feasts specific "forms," with additional meanings and special gifts of grace. Pentecost is distinguished from all the solemnities by its importance since what Jesus himself had announced as the purpose of the whole of his mission on earth is brought about in it. Indeed, on his way up to Jerusalem he had declared to his disciples: "I came to cast fire upon the earth; and would that it were already kindled!" (Lk 12:49). These words were most visibly brought about fifty days after the Resurrection, at Pentecost, the ancient Jewish feast which in the Church has become the feast par excellence of the Holy Spirit: "There appeared to them tongues as of fire ... and they were all filled with the Holy Spirit" (Acts 2:3–4). The real fire, the Holy Spirit, was brought to the earth by Christ. He did not steal it from the gods like Prometheus, according to the Greek myth, but rather made himself the mediator of the "gift of God," obtaining it for us with the greatest act of love in history: his death on the Cross.

God wants to continue giving this "fire" to every human generation and he is naturally free to do so as and when he wishes. He is spirit, and the Spirit "blows where he wills" (cf. Jn 3:8). However, there is a "normal way" which God himself chose "to cast fire upon the earth": this way is Jesus, his only-begotten Son, incarnate, dead, and risen. In his turn Jesus Christ constituted the Church as his Mystical Body so that she might extend his mission in history. "Receive the Holy Spirit," the Lord said to the Apostles on the evening of the Resurrection, accompanying these words with an expressive gesture: "he breathed" on them (cf. Jn 20:22). In this way he showed that he was communicating his Spirit to them, the Spirit of the Father and of the Son. Now, dear brothers and sisters, in today's solemnity scripture tells us once again how the community should be, how we should be in order to receive the gift of the Holy Spirit. In the account which describes the event of Pentecost, the sacred Author recalls that the disciples "were all together in one place." This "place" was the Cenacle, the "Upper Room" where Jesus had eaten the Last Supper with his Apostles, where he had appeared to them risen; that room which had become, so to speak, the "headquarters" of the nascent Church (cf. Acts 1:13). The Acts of the Apostles, however, rather than insisting on the physical place, intends to point out the inner attitude of the disciples: "All these with one accord devoted themselves to prayer" (Acts 1:14). Harmony among the disciples is thus the condition for the coming of the Holy Spirit; and a presupposition of harmony is prayer.

Dear brothers and sisters, this also applies to the Church today, it applies to us, who are gathered here. If we want to prevent Pentecost from being reduced to a mere rite or even an evocative commemoration but want it to be an actual event of salvation, we must prepare ourselves in devout expectation for the gift of God through humble and silent listening to his Word. Since Pentecost is renewed in our time, perhaps taking nothing from the freedom of God the Church should concentrate less on activities and be more dedicated to prayer. The Mother of the Church, Mary Most Holy, Bride of the Holy Spirit, teaches us this. This year Pentecost falls on the very last day of May on which the Feast of the Visitation is normally celebrated. That too was a sort of miniature "Pentecost" which caused joy and praise to well up in the hearts of Elizabeth and Mary, one barren and the other a virgin, who both became mothers through an extraordinary divine intervention (cf. Lk 1:41–45). The music and singing that accompany this liturgy help us likewise to be with one accord devoted to prayer, and for this I express my deep gratitude to the Cathedral Choir and the *Kammerorchester* of Cologne. Joseph Haydn's *Harmoniemesse* has very appropriately been chosen for this liturgy on the bicentenary of his death, the last of the "Masses" composed by the great musician and a sublime symphony to the glory of God. I address my most cordial greeting to all of you who are gathered here on this occasion.

In the account of Pentecost the Acts of the Apostles uses two important images to indicate the Holy Spirit: the image of the storm and the image of fire. Clearly, St. Luke has in mind the theophany of Sinai, recounted in the Books of Exodus (19:16–19) and Deuteronomy (4:10–12, 36). In the ancient world the storm was seen as a sign of divine power, before which man felt subjugated and terrified. However, I would like to emphasize another aspect too: the storm is described as a "mighty wind" and this makes one think of the air which distinguishes our planet from the other stars and enables us to live on it. What air is for biological life, the Holy Spirit is for spiritual life; and just as an atmospheric pollution exists that poisons the environment and living beings, thus a pollution of heart and spirit exists that mortifies and poisons spiritual life. In the same way that one must not become inured to the poisons in the air and for this reason ecological commitment is a priority today; likewise one must not become inured to what corrupts the mind. On the other hand it seems that it is not difficult to become accustomed to the many products that contaminate both the mind and the heart and that circulate in our society, for example, images which boost pleasure, violence, or contempt for men and women. This is also freedom, people say, without realizing that all this pollutes, and intoxicates the mind, especially that of the new generations and moreover ends by conditioning their very freedom. The metaphor of the mighty wind of Pentecost makes one think instead of how precious it is to breathe clean air, physically with the lungs and spiritually with the heart, the healthy air of the Spirit who is love!

The other image of the Holy Spirit which we find in the Acts of the Apostles is fire. I mentioned at the beginning the comparison between Jesus and the mythological figure of Prometheus which recalls a characteristic aspect of modern man. In possessing himself of the energies of the cosmos "fire" the human being seems today to assert himself as a god and to wish to transform the world, excluding, setting aside, or even rejecting the Creator of the universe. Man no longer wants to be an image of God but of himself; he declares himself autonomous, free, and adult. Of course, this attitude reveals a relationship with God which is not authentic, the consequence of a false image which has been fabricated of him, like the Prodigal Son in the Gospel parable who believes that he can fulfill himself by distancing himself from his father's house. In the hands of such a man "fire" and its enormous potential become dangerous: they can backfire against life and humanity itself, as history unfortunately shows. The tragedies of Hiroshima and Nagasaki, where atomic energy used for the purposes of war ended by sowing death on an unheard of scale, serve as a perennial warning.

It would truly be possible to find many examples, less grave but equally symptomatic, in everyday reality. Sacred scripture reveals to us that the energy capable of moving the world is not an anonymous and blind force but the action of the "Spirit of God... moving over the face of the waters" (Gn 1:2) at the beginning of the creation. And Jesus Christ "brought to the earth" not the vital force that already lived in it but the Holy Spirit, that is, the love of God who "renews the face of the earth," purifying it from evil and setting it free from the dominion of death (cf. Ps 103 [104]:29–30). This pure, essential, and personal "fire," the fire of love, came down upon the Apostles gathered in prayer with Mary in the Upper Room, to make the Church an extension of Christ's work of renewal.

Lastly, a final thought may also be found in the account of the Acts of the Apostles: the Holy Spirit overcomes fear. We know that the disciples sought shelter in the Upper Room after the arrest of their Lord and that they had remained isolated for fear of suffering the same fate. After Jesus' Resurrection their fear was not suddenly dispelled. But here at Pentecost, when the Holy Spirit rested upon them, those men emerged fearless and began to proclaim the Good News of the Crucified and Risen Christ to all. They were not afraid because they felt they were in the hands of the strongest One. Yes, dear brothers and sisters, wherever the Spirit of God enters he puts fear to flight; he makes us know and feel that we are in the hands of an Omnipotence of love: something happens, his infinite love does not abandon us. It is demonstrated by the witness of martyrs, by the courage of confessors of the faith, by the undaunted zeal of missionaries, by the frankness of preachers, by the example of all the saints, even some who were adolescents and children. It is demonstrated by the very existence of the Church which, despite the limitations and sins of men and women, continues to cross the ocean of history, blown by the breath of God and enlivened by his purifying fire. With this faith and joyful hope let us repeat today, through the intercession of Mary: *"Send forth your Spirit, O Lord, and renew the face of the earth."*

## The Protection of Creation

From General Audience,
August 26, 2009

The various phenomena of environmental degradation and natural disasters which, unfortunately, are often reported in the news remind us of the urgent need to respect nature as we should, recovering and appreciating a correct relationship with the environment in everyday life. A new sensitivity to these topics that justly give rise to concern on the part of the authorities and of public opinion is developing and is expressed in the increasing number of meetings, also at the international level.

The earth is indeed a precious gift of the Creator who, in designing its intrinsic order, has given us bearings that guide us as stewards of his creation. Precisely from within this framework, the Church considers matters concerning the environment and its protection intimately linked to the theme of integral human development. In my recent encyclical, *Caritas in Veritate,* I referred more than once to such questions, recalling the "pressing moral need for renewed solidarity"[12] not only between countries but also between individuals, since the natural environment is given by God to everyone, and our use of it entails a personal responsibility toward humanity as a whole, and in particular toward the poor and toward future generations.[13] Bearing in mind our common responsibility for creation,[14] the Church is not only committed to promoting the protection of land, water, and air as gifts of the Creator destined to everyone but above all she invites others and works herself to protect mankind from self-destruction. In fact, "when 'human ecology' is respected within society, environmental ecology also benefits."[15] Is it not true that an irresponsible use of creation begins precisely where God is marginalized or even denied? If the relationship between human creatures and the Creator is forgotten, matter is reduced

---

12. Benedict XVI, *Caritas in Veritate,* n. 49.
13. Cf. ibid., n. 48.       14. Cf. ibid., n. 51.
15. Ibid., n. 51.

to a selfish possession, man becomes the "last word," and the purpose of human existence is reduced to a scramble for the maximum number of possessions possible.

The created world, structured in an intelligent way by God, is entrusted to our responsibility and though we are able to analyze it and transform it we cannot consider ourselves creation's absolute master. We are called, rather, to exercise responsible stewardship of creation, in order to protect it, to enjoy its fruits, and to cultivate it, finding the resources necessary for everyone to live with dignity. Through the help of nature itself and through hard work and creativity, humanity is indeed capable of carrying out its grave duty to hand on the earth to future generations so that they too, in turn, will be able to inhabit it worthily and continue to cultivate it.[16] For this to happen, it is essential to develop "that covenant between human beings and the environment, which should mirror the creative love of God," recognizing that we all come from God and that we are all journeying toward him.[17] How important it is then, that the international community and individual governments send the right signals to their citizens to succeed in countering harmful ways of treating the environment! The economic and social costs of using up shared environmental resources must be recognized with transparency and borne by those who incur them, and not by other peoples or future generations. The protection of the environment, and the safeguarding of resources and of the climate, oblige all international leaders to act jointly respecting the law and promoting solidarity with the weakest regions of the

16. Cf. ibid., n. 50.
17. Benedict XVI, Message for the 2008 World Day of Peace, n. 7, January 1, 2008.

world.[18] Together we can build an integral human development beneficial for all peoples, present and future, a development inspired by the values of charity in truth. For this to happen it is essential that the current model of global development be transformed through a greater, and shared, acceptance of responsibility for creation: this is demanded not only by environmental factors, but also by the scandal of hunger and human misery.

Dear brothers and sisters, let us now give thanks to the Lord and make our own the words of St. Francis found in "The Canticle of All Creatures":

Most High, all-powerful, all-good Lord,
All praise is Yours, all glory, all honor and all blessings.
To you alone, Most High, do they belong.

So says St. Francis. We, too, wish to pray and live in the spirit of these words.

## The Keys to the Earth Are in the Hands of Man

From Address to a Group of Sponsors and Promoters
of the Holy See Pavilion at the 2008 International Exposition
in Zaragoza (Spain), September 10, 2009

The Holy See pavilion, one of the most visited and appreciated, housed an important exhibition of the valuable artistic, cultural, and religious patrimony that the Church looks after. The initiative aimed to offer its numerous visitors a timely re-

---

18. Cf. Benedict XVI, *Caritas in Veritate*, n. 50.

flection on the importance and fundamental value of water for human life.

Through its participation in the Zaragoza Expo, the Holy See sought not only to demonstrate the imperative need to protect the environment and nature constantly but also to discover their deepest spiritual and religious dimension. Today, as never before, it is essential to help people grasp that creation is something more than a simple source of wealth to be exploited by human hands. Indeed, when God, through creation, gave man the keys to the earth, he expected him to use this great gift properly, making it fruitful in a responsible and respectful way. The human being discovers the intrinsic value of nature if he learns to see it as it truly is, the expression of a project of love and truth which speaks to us of the Creator and of his love for humanity, which will find its fullness in Christ at the end of time.[19] In this regard, it is appropriate to recall once again the close relationship that exists between protection of the environment and respect for the ethical requirements of human nature, since "when the 'human ecology' is respected within society, environmental ecology also benefits."[20]

## Creation Is Marked by Finitude

From Angelus, November 15, 2009

This year, we have been accompanied along our itinerary through the Sunday biblical readings by St. Mark's Gospel,

19. Cf. ibid., n. 48.
20. Ibid., n. 51.

which today presents to us part of Jesus' discourse on the end of times. In this discourse is a phrase whose terse clarity is striking: "Heaven and earth will pass away, but my words will not pass away" (Mk 13:31). Let us pause a moment to reflect on this prophecy of Christ.

The expression "heaven and earth" recurs frequently in the Bible in reference to the whole universe, the entire cosmos. Jesus declares that all this is destined to "pass away"; not only the earth but also heaven, which here is meant in a purely cosmic sense and not as synonymous with God. Sacred scripture knows no ambiguity: all creation is marked by finitude, including the elements divinized by ancient mythologies; there is no confusion between creation and the Creator but rather a decided difference. With this clear distinction Jesus says that his words "will not pass away," that is to say they are part of God and therefore eternal. Even if they were spoken in the concreteness of his earthly existence, they are prophetic words par excellence, as Jesus affirms elsewhere, addressing the heavenly Father: "I have given them the words which you gave me, and they have received them and know in truth that I came from you; and they have believed that you sent me" (Jn 17:8). In a well-known parable Christ compares himself to the sower and explains that the seed is the word (cf. Mk 4:14); those who hear it, accept it, and bear fruit (cf. Mk 4:20) take part in the Kingdom of God, that is, they live under his lordship. They remain *in* the world, but are no longer *of* the world. They bear within them a seed of eternity, a principle of transformation that is already manifest now in a good life, enlivened by charity, and that in the end will produce the resurrection of the flesh. This is the power of Christ's word.

Dear friends, the Virgin Mary is the living sign of this truth. Her heart was "good soil" that received with complete willingness the Word of God, so that her whole life, transformed according to the image of the Son, was introduced into eternity, body and soul, in anticipation of the eternal vocation of every human being. Let us now make our own in prayer her response to the Angel: "Let it be to me according to your word" (Lk 1:38), so that in following Christ on the way of the Cross we too may be able to attain the glory of the Resurrection.

## If You Want to Cultivate Peace, Protect Creation

From Message for the Celebration of
the World Day of Peace,
January 1, 2010

1. At the beginning of this New Year, I wish to offer heartfelt greetings of peace to all Christian communities, international leaders, and people of good will throughout the world. For this forty-third World Day of Peace I have chosen the theme: "If You Want to Cultivate Peace, Protect Creation." Respect for creation is of immense consequence, not least because "creation is the beginning and the foundation of all God's works" and its preservation has now become essential for the pacific coexistence of mankind.[21] Man's inhumanity to man has given rise to numerous threats to peace and to authentic and integral human development—wars, international and regional conflicts, acts of ter-

21. *Catechism of the Catholic Church* (1993), n. 198.

rorism, and violations of human rights. Yet no less troubling are the threats arising from the neglect—if not downright misuse—of the earth and the natural goods that God has given us. For this reason, it is imperative that mankind renew and strengthen "that covenant between human beings and the environment, which should mirror the creative love of God, from whom we come and toward whom we are journeying."[22]

2. In my encyclical *Caritas in Veritate,* I noted that integral human development is closely linked to the obligations which flow from *man's relationship with the natural environment.* The environment must be seen as God's gift to all people, and the use we make of it entails a shared responsibility for all humanity, especially the poor and future generations. I also observed that whenever nature, and human beings in particular, are seen merely as products of chance or an evolutionary determinism, our overall sense of responsibility wanes.[23] On the other hand, seeing creation as God's gift to humanity helps us understand our vocation and worth as human beings. With the psalmist, we can exclaim with wonder: "When I look at your heavens, the work of your hands, the moon and the stars which you have established; what is man that you are mindful of him, and the son of man that you care for him?" (Ps 8:4–5). Contemplating the beauty of creation inspires us to recognize the love of the Creator, that Love which "moves the sun and the other stars."[24]

3. Twenty years ago, Pope John Paul II devoted his Message for the World Day of Peace to the theme: "Peace with God the

22. Benedict XVI, Message for the 2008 World Day of Peace, n. 7, January 1, 2008.
23. Cf. Benedict XVI, *Caritas in Veritate,* n. 48.
24. Dante Alighieri, *Paradiso,* Canto 33.145.

Creator, Peace with All of Creation." He emphasized our relationship, as God's creatures, with the universe all around us. "In our day," he wrote, "there is a growing awareness that world peace is threatened... also by a lack of *due respect for nature.*" He added that *"ecological awareness,* rather than being downplayed, needs to be helped to develop and mature, and find fitting expression in concrete programs and initiatives."[25] Previous popes had spoken of the relationship between human beings and the environment. In 1971, for example, on the eightieth anniversary of Leo XIII's encyclical *Rerum Novarum,* Paul VI pointed out that "by an ill-considered exploitation of nature (man) risks destroying it and becoming in his turn the victim of this degradation." He added that "not only is the material environment becoming a permanent menace—pollution and refuse, new illnesses, and absolute destructive capacity—but the human framework is no longer under man's control, thus creating an environment for tomorrow which may well be intolerable. This is a wide-ranging social problem which concerns the entire human family."[26]

4. Without entering into the merit of specific technical solutions, the Church is nonetheless concerned, as an "expert in humanity," to call attention to the relationship between the Creator, human beings, and the created order. In 1990 John Paul II had spoken of an "ecological crisis" and, in highlighting its primarily ethical character, pointed to the "urgent moral need for a new solidarity."[27] His appeal is all the more pressing today, in the face of signs of a growing crisis which it would be irrespon-

25. John Paul II, Message for the 1990 World Day of Peace, n. 1, January 1, 1990.

26. Paul VI, Apostolic Letter *Octogesima Adveniens* (May 14, 1971), n. 21.

27. John Paul II, Message for the 1990 World Day of Peace, n. 10, January 1, 1990.

sible not to take seriously. Can we remain indifferent before the problems associated with such realities as climate change, desertification, the deterioration and loss of productivity in vast agricultural areas, the pollution of rivers and aquifers, the loss of biodiversity, the increase of natural catastrophes, and the deforestation of equatorial and tropical regions? Can we disregard the growing phenomenon of "environmental refugees," people who are forced by the degradation of their natural habitat to forsake it—and often their possessions as well—in order to face the dangers and uncertainties of forced displacement? Can we remain impassive in the face of actual and potential conflicts involving access to natural resources? All these are issues with a profound impact on the exercise of human rights, such as the right to life, food, health, and development.

5. It should be evident that the ecological crisis cannot be viewed in isolation from other related questions, since it is closely linked to the notion of development itself and our understanding of man in his relationship to others and to the rest of creation. Prudence would thus dictate a *profound, long-term review of our model of development,* one which would take into consideration the meaning of the economy and its goals with an eye to correcting its malfunctions and misapplications. The ecological health of the planet calls for this, but it is also demanded by the cultural and moral crisis of humanity whose symptoms have for some time been evident in every part of the world.[28] Humanity needs a *profound cultural renewal;* it needs to *rediscover those values which can serve as the solid basis* for building a brighter future for

28. Cf. Benedict XVI, *Caritas in Veritate,* n. 32.

all. Our present crises—be they economic, food-related, environmental, or social—are ultimately also moral crises, and all of them are interrelated. They require us to rethink the path which we are travelling together. Specifically, they call for a lifestyle marked by sobriety and solidarity, with new rules and forms of engagement, one which focuses confidently and courageously on strategies that actually work, while decisively rejecting those that have failed. Only in this way can the current crisis become an *opportunity for discernment and new strategic planning.*

6. Is it not true that what we call "nature" in a cosmic sense has its origin in "a plan of love and truth"? The world "is not the product of any necessity whatsoever, nor of blind fate or chance.... The world proceeds from the free will of God; he wanted to make his creatures share in his being, in his intelligence, and in his goodness."[29] The Book of Genesis, in its very first pages, points to the wise design of the cosmos: it comes forth from God's mind and finds its culmination in man and woman, made in the image and likeness of the Creator to "fill the earth" and to "have dominion over" it as "stewards" of God himself (cf. Gn 1:28). The harmony between the Creator, mankind, and the created world, as described by sacred scripture, was disrupted by the sin of Adam and Eve, by man and woman, who wanted to take the place of God and refused to acknowledge that they were his creatures. As a result, the work of "exercising dominion" over the earth, "tilling it and keeping it," was also disrupted, and conflict arose within and between mankind and the rest of creation (cf. Gn 3:17–19). Human be-

29. *Catechism of the Catholic Church* (1993), n. 295.

ings let themselves be mastered by selfishness; they misunderstood the meaning of God's command and exploited creation out of a desire to exercise absolute domination over it. But the true meaning of God's original command, as the Book of Genesis clearly shows, was not a simple conferral of authority, but rather a summons to responsibility. The wisdom of the ancients had recognized that nature is not at our disposal as "a heap of scattered refuse."[30] Biblical revelation made us see that nature is a gift of the Creator, who gave it an inbuilt order and enabled man to draw from it the principles needed to "till it and keep it" (cf. Gn. 2:15).[31] Everything that exists belongs to God, who has entrusted it to man, albeit not for his arbitrary use. Once man, instead of acting as God's co-worker, sets himself up in place of God, he ends up provoking a rebellion on the part of nature, "which is more tyrannized than governed by him."[32] Man thus has a duty to exercise responsible stewardship over creation, to care for it and to cultivate it.[33]

7. Sad to say, it is all too evident that large numbers of people in different countries and areas of our planet are experiencing increased hardship because of the negligence or refusal of many others to exercise responsible stewardship over the environment. The Second Vatican Ecumenical Council reminded us that "God has destined the earth and everything it contains for all peoples and nations."[34] The goods of creation belong to

30. Heraclitus of Ephesus, Fragment 22B124, in Hermann Diels and Walther Kranz, *Die Fragmente der Vorsokratiker,* 6th ed. (Berlin: Weidmann, 1952).

31. Cf. Benedict XVI, *Caritas in Veritate,* n. 48.

32. John Paul II, *Centesimus Annus,* n. 37.

33. Cf. Benedict XVI, *Caritas in Veritate,* n. 50.

34. Second Vatican Council, *Gaudium et Spes,* n. 69.

humanity as a whole. Yet the current pace of environmental exploitation is seriously endangering the supply of certain natural resources not only for the present generation, but above all for generations yet to come.[35] It is not hard to see that environmental degradation is often due to the lack of far-sighted official policies or to the pursuit of myopic economic interests, which then, tragically, become a serious threat to creation. To combat this phenomenon, economic activity needs to consider the fact that "every economic decision has a moral consequence" and thus show increased respect for the environment.[36] When making use of natural resources, we should be concerned for their protection and consider the cost entailed—environmentally and socially—as an essential part of the overall expenses incurred. The international community and national governments are responsible for sending the right signals in order to combat effectively the misuse of the environment. To protect the environment, and to safeguard natural resources and the climate, there is a need to act in accordance with clearly defined rules, also from the juridical and economic standpoint, while at the same time taking into due account the solidarity we owe to those living in the poorer areas of our world and to future generations.

8. *A greater sense of intergenerational solidarity* is urgently needed. Future generations cannot be saddled with the cost of our use of common environmental resources. "We have inherited from past generations, and we have benefited from the work of our contemporaries; for this reason we have obligations toward all, and we cannot refuse to interest ourselves in those who will

35. Cf. John Paul II, *Sollicitudo Rei Socialis*, n. 34.
36. Benedict XVI, *Caritas in Veritate*, n. 37.

come after us, to enlarge the human family. Universal solidarity represents a benefit as well as a duty. *This is a responsibility that present generations have toward those of the future,* a responsibility that also concerns individual States and the international community."[37] Natural resources should be used in such a way that immediate benefits do not have a negative impact on living creatures, human and not, present and future; that the protection of private property does not conflict with the universal destination of goods;[38] that human activity does not compromise the fruitfulness of the earth, for the benefit of people now and in the future. In addition to a fairer sense of intergenerational solidarity there is also an urgent moral need for a renewed sense of *intragenerational solidarity,* especially in relationships between developing countries and highly industrialized countries: "The international community has an urgent duty to find institutional means of regulating the exploitation of non-renewable resources, involving poor countries in the process, in order to plan together for the future."[39] *The ecological crisis shows the urgency of a solidarity which embraces time and space.* It is important to acknowledge that among the causes of the present ecological crisis is the historical responsibility of the industrialized countries. Yet the less developed countries, and emerging countries in particular, are not exempt from their own responsibilities with regard to creation, for the duty of gradually adopting effective environmental measures and policies is incumbent upon all. This would be accomplished more easily if self-interest played a lesser

37. *Compendium of the Social Doctrine of the Church,* n. 467; cf. Paul VI, *Populorum Progressio,* n. 17.

38. Cf. John Paul II, *Centesimus Annus,* nn. 30–31, 43.

39. Benedict XVI, *Caritas in Veritate,* n. 49.

role in the granting of aid and the sharing of knowledge and cleaner technologies.

9. To be sure, among the basic problems which the international community has to address is that of energy resources and the development of joint and sustainable strategies to satisfy the energy needs of the present and future generations. This means that technologically advanced societies must be prepared to encourage more sober lifestyles, while reducing their energy consumption and improving its efficiency. At the same time there is a need to encourage research into, and utilization of, forms of energy with lower impact on the environment and "a worldwide redistribution of energy resources, so that countries lacking those resources can have access to them."[40] The ecological crisis offers a historic opportunity to develop a common plan of action aimed at orienting the model of global development toward greater respect for creation and for an integral human development inspired by the values proper to charity in truth. I would advocate the adoption of a model of development based on the centrality of the human person, on the promotion and sharing of the common good, on responsibility, on a realization of our need for a changed lifestyle, and on prudence, the virtue which tells us what needs to be done today in view of what might happen tomorrow.[41]

10. A sustainable comprehensive management of the environment and the resources of the planet demands that human intelligence be directed to technological and scientific research and its practical applications. The "new solidarity" for which

40. Ibid.
41. Cf. St. Thomas Aquinas, *Summa Theologiae* II–II, q. 49, a. 5.

John Paul II called in his Message for the 1990 World Day of Peace[42] and the "global solidarity" for which I myself appealed in my Message for the 2009 World Day of Peace are essential attitudes in shaping our efforts to protect creation through a better internationally coordinated management of the earth's resources, particularly today, when there is an increasingly clear link between combatting environmental degradation and promoting an integral human development. These two realities are inseparable, since "the integral development of individuals necessarily entails a joint effort for the development of humanity as a whole."[43] At present there are a number of scientific developments and innovative approaches which promise to provide satisfactory and balanced solutions to the problem of our relationship to the environment. Encouragement needs to be given, for example, to research into effective ways of exploiting the immense potential of solar energy. Similar attention also needs to be paid to the worldwide problem of water and to the global water cycle system, which is of prime importance for life on earth and whose stability could be seriously jeopardized by climate change. Suitable strategies for rural development centered on small farmers and their families should be explored, as well as the implementation of appropriate policies for the management of forests, for waste disposal, and for strengthening the linkage between combatting climate change and overcoming poverty. Ambitious national policies are required, together with a necessary international commitment which will offer important benefits especially in the medium and long term. There is a need,

42. John Paul II, Message for the 1990 World Day of Peace, n. 9, January 1, 1990.
43. Paul VI, *Populorum Progressio*, n. 43.

in effect, to move beyond a purely consumerist mentality in order to promote forms of agricultural and industrial production capable of respecting creation and satisfying the primary needs of all. The ecological problem must be dealt with not only because of the chilling prospects of environmental degradation on the horizon; the real motivation must be the quest for authentic worldwide solidarity inspired by the values of charity, justice, and the common good. For that matter, as I have stated elsewhere, "technology is never merely technology. It reveals man and his aspirations toward development; it expresses the inner tension that impels him gradually to overcome material limitations. *Technology in this sense is a response to God's command to till and keep the land* (cf. Gn 2:15) that he has entrusted to humanity, and it must serve to reinforce the covenant between human beings and the environment, a covenant that should mirror God's creative love."[44]

11. It is becoming more and more evident that the issue of environmental degradation challenges us to examine our lifestyle and the prevailing models of consumption and production, which are often unsustainable from a social, environmental, and even economic point of view. We can no longer do without a real change of outlook which will result in *new lifestyles,* "in which the quest for truth, beauty, goodness, and communion with others for the sake of common growth are the factors which determine consumer choices, savings, and investments."[45] Education for peace must increasingly begin with far-reaching decisions on the part of individuals, families, communities, and states. We

44. Benedict XVI, *Caritas in Veritate*, n. 69.
45. John Paul II, *Centesimus Annus*, n. 36.

are all responsible for the protection and care of the environment. This responsibility knows no boundaries. In accordance with the *principle of subsidiarity* it is important for everyone to be committed at his or her proper level, working to overcome the prevalence of particular interests. A special role in raising awareness and information belongs to the different groups present in civil society and to the non-governmental organizations which work with determination and generosity for the spread of ecological responsibility, responsibility which should be ever more deeply anchored in respect for "human ecology." The media also have a responsibility in this regard to offer positive and inspiring models. In a word, concern for the environment calls for a broad global vision of the world; a responsible common effort to move beyond approaches based on selfish nationalistic interests toward a vision constantly open to the needs of all peoples. We cannot remain indifferent to what is happening around us, for the deterioration of any one part of the planet affects us all. Relationships between individuals, social groups, and states, like those between human beings and the environment, must be marked by respect and "charity in truth." In this broader context one can only encourage the efforts of the international community to ensure progressive disarmament and a world free of nuclear weapons, whose presence alone threatens the life of the planet and the ongoing integral development of the present generation and of generations yet to come.

12. *The Church has a responsibility toward creation,* and she considers it her duty to exercise that responsibility in public life, in order to protect earth, water, and air as gifts of God the Creator meant for everyone, and above all to save mankind from the

danger of self-destruction. The degradation of nature is closely linked to the cultural models shaping human coexistence: consequently, "when 'human ecology' is respected within society, environmental ecology also benefits."[46] Young people cannot be asked to respect the environment if they are not helped, within families and society as a whole, to respect themselves. The book of nature is one and indivisible; it includes not only the environment but also individual, family, and social ethics.[47] Our duties toward the environment flow from our duties toward the person, considered both individually and in relation to others.

Hence I readily encourage efforts to promote a greater sense of ecological responsibility which, as I indicated in my encyclical *Caritas in Veritate,* would safeguard an authentic "human ecology" and thus forcefully reaffirm the inviolability of human life at every stage and in every condition, the dignity of the person and the unique mission of the family, where one is trained in love of neighbor and respect for nature.[48] There is a need to safeguard the human patrimony of society. This patrimony of values originates in and is part of the natural moral law, which is the foundation of respect for the human person and creation.

13. Nor must we forget the very significant fact that many people experience peace and tranquility, renewal and reinvigoration, when they come into close contact with the beauty and harmony of nature. There exists a certain reciprocity: as we care for creation, we realize that God, through creation, cares for us. On the other hand, a correct understanding of the relationship

46. Benedict XVI, *Caritas in Veritate,* n. 51.
47. Cf. ibid., nn. 15, 51.
48. Ibid., nn. 28, 51, 61; cf. John Paul II, *Centesimus Annus,* nn. 38, 39.

between man and the environment will not end by absolutizing nature or by considering it more important than the human person. If the Church's magisterium expresses grave misgivings about notions of the environment inspired by ecocentrism and biocentrism, it is because such notions eliminate the difference of identity and worth between the human person and other living things. In the name of a supposedly egalitarian vision of the "dignity" of all living creatures, such notions end up abolishing the distinctiveness and superior role of human beings. They also open the way to a new pantheism tinged with neopaganism, which would see the source of man's salvation in nature alone, understood in purely naturalistic terms. The Church, for her part, is concerned that the question be approached in a balanced way, with respect for the "grammar" which the Creator has inscribed in his handiwork by giving man the role of a steward and administrator with responsibility over creation, a role which man must certainly not abuse, but also one which he may not abdicate. In the same way, the opposite position, which would absolutize technology and human power, results in a grave assault not only on nature, but also on human dignity itself.[49]

14. *If you want to cultivate peace, protect creation.* The quest for peace by people of goodwill surely would become easier if all acknowledge the indivisible relationship between God, human beings, and the whole of creation. In the light of divine revelation and in fidelity to the Church's tradition, Christians have their own contribution to make. They contemplate the cosmos

49. Cf. Benedict XVI, *Caritas in Veritate*, n. 70.

and its marvels in light of the creative work of the Father and the redemptive work of Christ, who by his death and Resurrection has reconciled with God "all things, whether on earth or in heaven" (Col 1:20). Christ, crucified and risen, has bestowed his Spirit of holiness upon mankind, to guide the course of history in anticipation of that day when, with the glorious return of the Savior, there will be "new heavens and a new earth" (2 Pt 3:13), in which justice and peace will dwell forever. Protecting the natural environment in order to build a world of peace is thus a duty incumbent upon each and all. It is an urgent challenge, one to be faced with renewed and concerted commitment; it is also a providential opportunity to hand down to coming generations the prospect of a better future for all. May this be clear to world leaders and to those at every level who are concerned for the future of humanity: the protection of creation and peacemaking are profoundly linked! For this reason, I invite all believers to raise a fervent prayer to God, the all-powerful Creator and the Father of mercies, so that all men and women may take to heart the urgent appeal: *If you want to cultivate peace, protect creation.*

## The Protection of Creation, an Element of Peace and of Justice

From Address to the Members of the Diplomatic Corps
for the Traditional Exchange of New Year Greetings,
January 11, 2010

The Church is open to everyone because, in God, she lives for others! She thus shares deeply in the fortunes of humanity, which in this new year continues to be marked by the dramatic crisis of the global economy and consequently a serious and widespread social instability. In my encyclical *Caritas in Veritate,* I invited everyone to look to the deeper causes of this situation: in the last analysis, they are to be found in a current self-centered and materialistic way of thinking which fails to acknowledge the limitations inherent in every creature. Today I would like to stress that the same way of thinking also endangers creation. Each of us could probably cite an example of the damage that this has caused to the environment the world over. I will offer an example, from any number of others, taken from the recent history of Europe. Twenty years ago, after the fall of the Berlin wall and the collapse of the materialistic and atheistic regimes which had for several decades dominated a part of this continent, was it not easy to assess the great harm which an economic system lacking any reference to the truth about man had done not only to the dignity and freedom of individuals and peoples, but to nature itself, by polluting soil, water, and air? The denial of God distorts the freedom of the human person, yet it also devastates creation. It follows that the protection of creation is not principally a response to an aesthetic need, but much more to a moral need, in as much as nature expresses a plan of love and truth which is prior to us and which comes from God.

For this reason I share the growing concern caused by economic and political resistance to combatting the degradation of the environment. This problem was evident even recently, during the fifteenth Session of the Conference of the States Parties to the United Nations Framework Convention on Climate Change held in Copenhagen from 7 to 18 December last. I trust that in the course of this year, first in Bonn and later in Mexico City, it will be possible to reach an agreement for effectively dealing with this question. The issue is all the more important in that the very future of some nations is at stake, particularly some island states.

It is proper, however, that this concern and commitment for the environment should be situated within the larger framework of the great challenges now facing mankind. If we wish to build true peace, how can we separate, or even set at odds, the protection of the environment and the protection of human life, including the life of the unborn? It is in man's respect for himself that his sense of responsibility for creation is shown. As St. Thomas Aquinas has taught, man represents all that is most noble in the universe.[50] Furthermore, as I noted during the recent Food and Agriculture Organization (FAO) World Summit on Food Security, "the world has enough food for all its inhabitants" provided that selfishness does not lead some to hoard the goods which are intended for all.[51]

I would like to stress again that the protection of creation calls for an appropriate management of the natural resources of different countries and, in the first place, of those which are economically disadvantaged. I think of the continent of Africa, which I had the joy of visiting last March during my journey to Cameroon and Angola, and which was the subject of the deliberations of the recent Special Assembly of the Synod of Bishops. The synod fathers pointed with concern to the erosion and

50. Cf. St. Thomas Aquinas, *Summa Theologiae* I, q. 29, a. 3.
51. Benedict XVI, Address to FAO on the Occasion of the World Summit on Food Security, n. 2, Rome, November 16, 2009.

desertification of large tracts of arable land as a result of over-exploitation and environmental pollution.[52] In Africa, as elsewhere, there is a need to make political and economic decisions which ensure "forms of agricultural and industrial production capable of respecting creation and satisfying the primary needs of all."[53]

How can we forget, for that matter, that the struggle for access to natural resources is one of the causes of a number of conflicts, not least in Africa, as well as a continuing threat elsewhere? For this reason too, I forcefully repeat that to cultivate peace, one must protect creation! Furthermore, there are still large areas, for example in Afghanistan or in some countries of Latin America, where agriculture is unfortunately still linked to the production of narcotics, and is a not insignificant source of employment and income. If we want peace, we need to preserve creation by rechanneling these activities; I once more urge the international community not to become resigned to the drug trade and the grave moral and social problems which it creates.

Ladies and gentlemen, the protection of creation is indeed an important element of peace and justice! Among the many challenges which it presents, one of the most serious is increased military spending and the cost of maintaining and developing nuclear arsenals. Enormous resources are being consumed for these purposes, when they could be spent on the development of peoples, especially those who are poorest. For this reason I firmly hope that, during the Nuclear Non-Proliferation Treaty

52. Second Special Assembly for Africa of the Synod of Bishops, Final List of Propositions (October 23, 2009), Proposition 22.

53. Benedict XVI, Message for the 2010 World Day of Peace, n. 10, January 1, 2010.

Review Conference to be held this May in New York, concrete decisions will be made toward progressive disarmament, with a view to freeing our planet from nuclear arms. More generally, I deplore the fact that arms production and export helps to perpetuate conflicts and violence, as in Darfur, in Somalia, or in the Democratic Republic of the Congo. Together with the inability of the parties directly involved to step back from the spiral of violence and pain spawned by these conflicts, there is the apparent powerlessness of other countries and the international organizations to restore peace, to say nothing of the indifference, amounting practically to resignation, of public opinion worldwide. There is no need to insist on the extent to which such conflicts damage and degrade the environment. Finally, how can I fail to mention terrorism, which endangers countless innocent lives and generates widespread anxiety. On this solemn occasion, I would like to renew the appeal which I made during the Angelus prayer of 1 January last to all those belonging to armed groups, of whatever kind, to abandon the path of violence and to open their hearts to the joy of peace.

The grave acts of violence to which I have just alluded, combined with the scourges of poverty, hunger, natural disasters, and the destruction of the environment, have helped to swell the ranks of those who migrate from their native land. Given the extent of this exodus, I wish to exhort the various civil authorities to carry on their work with justice, solidarity, and foresight. Here I wish to speak in particular of the Christians of the Middle East. Beleaguered in various ways, even in the exercise of their religious freedom, they are leaving the land of their forebears, where the Church took root during the earliest centuries. To offer them encouragement and to make them feel the closeness of their brothers and sisters in faith, I have convened for next autumn a Special Assembly of the Synod of Bishops on the Middle East.

Ladies and gentlemen, to this point I have alluded only to a few aspects of the problem of the environment. Yet the causes of the situation which is now evident to everyone are of the moral order, and the question must be faced within the framework of a great program of education aimed at promoting an effective change of thinking and at creating new lifestyles. The community of believers can and wants to take part in this, but, for it to do so, its public role must be recognized. Sadly, in certain countries, mainly in the West, one increasingly encounters in political and cultural circles, as well in the media, scarce respect and at times hostility, if not scorn, directed toward religion and toward Christianity in particular. It is clear that if relativism is considered an essential element of democracy, one risks viewing secularity solely in the sense of excluding or, more precisely, denying the social importance of religion. But such an approach creates confrontation and division, disturbs peace, harms human ecology and, by rejecting in principle approaches other than its own, finishes in a dead end. There is thus an urgent need to delineate a positive and open secularity which, grounded in the just autonomy of the temporal order and the spiritual order, can foster healthy cooperation and a spirit of shared responsibility. Here I think of Europe, which, now that the Lisbon Treaty has taken effect, has entered a new phase in its process of integration, a process which the Holy See will continue to follow with close attention. Noting with satisfaction that the treaty provides for the European Union to maintain an "open, transparent, and regular" dialogue with the Churches,[54] I express my hope that in building its future, Europe will always draw upon the wellsprings of its Christian identity. As I said during my apostolic visit last September to the Czech Republic, Europe has an irreplaceable role to play "for the formation of the conscience of each generation and the promotion of a basic ethical consensus that serves every person who calls this continent 'home.'"[55]

To carry our reflection further, we must remember that the problem of the environment is complex; one might compare it to a multifaceted prism. Creatures differ from one another and can be protected, or endangered, in different ways, as we know from daily experience. One such attack comes from laws or proposals which, in the name of fighting discrimination, strike at the biological basis of the difference between the sexes. I am thinking, for example, of certain countries in Europe or North and South America. St. Columban stated that: "If you take away freedom, you take away dignity."[56] Yet freedom cannot be absolute, since man is not himself God, but the image of God, God's creation. For man, the path to be taken cannot be determined by caprice or willfulness, but must rather correspond to the structure willed by the Creator.

The protection of creation also entails other challenges, which can only be met by international solidarity. I think of the

54. Treaty of Lisbon, December 13, 2007, art. 17.

55. Benedict XVI, Meeting with the Civil and Political Authorities and with the Members of the Diplomatic Corps, Apostolic Journey to the Czech Republic, Prague, September 26, 2009.

56. St. Columban, Letter 4 to Attala, in *Sancti Columbani Opera* (Dublin: Dublin Institute for Advanced Studies, 1957), 34.

natural disasters which this past year have sown death, suffering, and destruction in the Philippines, Vietnam, Laos, Cambodia, and Taiwan. Nor can I pass over Indonesia and, closer to us, the Abruzzi region, hit by devastating earthquakes. Faced with events like these, generous aid should never be lacking, since the life itself of God's children is at stake. Yet, in addition to solidarity, the protection of creation also calls for concord and stability between states. Whenever disagreements and conflicts arise among them, in order to defend peace they must tenaciously pursue the path of constructive dialogue. This is what happened twenty-five years ago with the Treaty of Peace and Friendship between Argentina and Chile, reached thanks to the mediation of the Apostolic See. That treaty has borne abundant fruit in cooperation and prosperity which have in some way benefited all of Latin America. In this same area of the world, I am pleased by the rapprochement upon which Columbia and Ecuador have embarked after several months of tension. Closer to us, I am gratified by the agreement concluded between Croatia and Slovenia on arbitration regarding their sea and land borders. I am also pleased by the accord between Armenia and Turkey for the re-establishment of diplomatic relations, and I express my hope that, through dialogue, relations will improve among all the countries of the southern Caucasus. In the course of my pilgrimage to the Holy Land, I urgently appealed to the Israelis and the Palestinians to dialogue and to respect each others' rights. Once again I call for a universal recognition of the right of the State of Israel to exist and to enjoy peace and security within internationally recognized borders. Likewise, the right of the Palestinian people to a sovereign and independent homeland, to live in dignity and to enjoy freedom of movement, ought to be recognized. I would also like to request the support of everyone for the protection of the identity and sacred character of Jerusalem, and of its cultural and religious heritage, which is of universal value. Only thus will this unique city, holy yet deeply afflicted, be a sign and harbinger of that peace which God desires for the whole human family. Out of love for the dialogue and peace which protect creation, I exhort the government leaders and the citizens of Iraq to overcome their divisions and the temptation to violence and intolerance, in order to build together the future of their country. The Christian communities also wish to make their own contribution, but if this is to happen, they need to be assured respect, security, and freedom. Pakistan has been also hard hit by violence in recent months and certain episodes were directly aimed at the Christian minority. I ask that everything be done to avoid the re-occurrence of such acts of aggression, and to ensure that Christians feel fully a part of the life of their country. In speaking of acts of violence against Christians, I cannot fail to mention also the deplorable attack which the Egyptian Coptic community suffered in recent days, during its celebration of Christmas. Concerning Iran, I express my hope that through dialogue and cooperation joint solutions will be found on the national as well as the international level. I encourage Lebanon, which has emerged from a lengthy political crisis, to continue along the path of concord. I hope that Honduras, after a period of uncertainty and unrest, will move toward a recovery of normal political and social life. I desire the same for Guinea and Madagascar with the effective and disinterested aid of the international community.

Ladies and gentlemen, at the end of this rapid overview which, due to its brevity, cannot mention every situation worthy of note, I am reminded of the words of the Apostle Paul, for whom "all creation groans and is in agony" and "we ourselves groan inwardly" (Rom 8:20–23). There is so much suffering in our world, and human selfishness continues in many ways to harm creation. For this reason, the yearning for salvation which affects all creation is that much more intense and present in the hearts of all men and women, believers and non-believers alike. The Church points out that the response to this aspiration is Christ, "the firstborn of all creation, for in him all things in heaven and on earth were created" (Col 1:15–16). Looking to him, I exhort every person of good will to work confidently and generously for the sake of human dignity and freedom. May the light and strength of Jesus help us to respect human ecology, in the knowledge that natural ecology will likewise benefit, since the book of nature is one and indivisible. In this way we will be able to build peace, today and for the sake of generations to come.

## The Word of God and the Protection of Creation

From Post-Synodal Apostolic Exhortation *Verbum Domini* to the Bishops, Clergy, Consecrated Persons, and the Lay Faithful on the Word of God in the Life and Mission of the Church, September 30, 2010

108. Engagement with the world, as demanded by God's word, makes us look with new eyes at the entire created cosmos, which contains traces of that word through whom all things were

made (cf. Jn 1:2). As men and women who believe in and proclaim the Gospel, we have a responsibility toward creation. Revelation makes known God's plan for the cosmos, yet it also leads us to denounce that mistaken attitude which refuses to view all created realities as a reflection of their Creator, but instead as mere raw material, to be exploited without scruple. Man thus lacks that essential humility which would enable him to see creation as a gift from God, to be received and used in accordance with his plan. Instead, the arrogance of human beings who live "as if God did not exist" leads them to exploit and disfigure nature, failing to see it as the handiwork of the creative word. In this theological context, I would like to echo the statements of the synod fathers who reminded us that "accepting the word of God, attested to by scripture and by the Church's living tradition, gives rise to a new way of seeing things, promotes an authentic ecology which has its deepest roots in the obedience of faith ... [and] develops a renewed theological sensitivity to the goodness of all things, which are created in Christ."[57] We need to be re-educated in wonder and in the ability to recognize the beauty made manifest in created realities.[58]

57. XII Ordinary General Assembly of the Synod of Bishops, Final List of Propositions (October 25, 2008), Proposition 54.

58. Cf. Benedict XVI, Post-Synodal Apostolic Exhortation *Sacramentum Caritatis* (February 22, 2007), n. 92.

## In Contemplating Creation Man Has a Profound Sense of Gratitude and Recognition, but Also of Responsibility for Tilling and Keeping the Work of God

From Address to Representatives of the Italian
Ski Instructors, November 15, 2010

Sports are one of the means that contribute to the person's harmonious development and to his moral perfection.[59] Your duty as "ski instructors" helps to stimulate various capacities, for example, for persistence in pursuing goals, for respecting rules, and for tenacity in confronting and surmounting difficulties. Practiced ethically and with passion, sports become a training ground for learning and developing human and Christian values, as well as for practicing a healthy spirit of competition. In fact, they teach the harmonization of important dimensions of the human being, favoring their integral development. Through sports, a person understands better that his body cannot be considered an object; rather, through corporeity, he expresses himself and enters into relationships with others. In this way, the balance between the physical and spiritual dimensions does not bring us to idolize the body, but rather to respect it and not to let it become an instrument to be strengthened at all costs, possibly even by resorting to illegal methods.

The other aspect I would like to mention is suggested by the

59. Cf. Second Vatican Council, Declaration *Gravissimum Educationis* (October 28, 1965), n. 4.

fact that skiing is done in a mountain environment. This makes us feel small in a special way and restores for us the right dimensions of our being creatures. It enables us to ask ourselves about the meaning of creation and to look up on high and open ourselves to the Creator.

I think of how often, in climbing a mountain in order to ski down it or in cross-country skiing, breathtaking views unfolded; they uplift the mind and spontaneously invite us not only to raise our outer gaze but also the gaze of the heart.

In contemplating creation, man recognizes the greatness of God, the ultimate source of his being and of the universe. We should not forget that the relationship with creation is an important element for the development of the human identity and not even the sin of man has eliminated his duty to be a guardian of the world.

Sports can also be conceived and lived as a part of this responsibility. Progress in the fields of science and technology give human beings the possibility to meddle with and manipulate nature, but the risk that always lies in wait is the desire to replace the Creator and reduce creation to a product to be used and consumed.

What, instead, is the right approach? Surely it consists in a profound sense of gratitude and recognition, but also of responsibility for tilling and keeping the work of God (cf. Gn 2:15). Sports are a help in pursuing certain goals since they affect one's lifestyle itself which they orient to balance, self-discipline, and respect. For you, then, in particular, contact with nature is a reason for cultivating a profound love for God's creation.

In the light of these reflections, your role appears important for a healthy training in sports and an education in respect for the environment. This is not, therefore, a duty to carry out on one's own, but rather in agreement with families—especially when your students are minors—and in collaboration with school and other educational institutions. Your example as lay faithful is also important in the context of sports, which can give the right centrality to moments fundamental to the life of faith and, especially, to the sanctification of Sunday as the Lord's Day.

❦

## The World Is a Product of Creative Reason

From Easter Vigil Homily,
April 23, 2011

The liturgical celebration of the Easter Vigil makes use of two eloquent signs. First there is the fire that becomes light. As the procession makes its way through the church, shrouded in the darkness of the night, the light of the paschal candle becomes a wave of lights, and it speaks to us of Christ as the true morning star that never sets—the Risen Lord in whom light has conquered darkness. The second sign is water. On the one hand, it recalls the waters of the Red Sea, decline and death, the mystery of the Cross. But now it is presented to us as spring water, a life-giving element amid the dryness. Thus it becomes the image of the sacrament of Baptism, through which we become sharers in the death and Resurrection of Jesus Christ.

Yet these great signs of creation, light and water, are not the only constituent elements of the liturgy of the Easter Vigil. Another essential feature is the ample encounter with the words of sacred scripture that it provides. Before the liturgical reform there were twelve Old Testament readings and two from the New Testament. The New Testament readings have been retained. The number of Old Testament readings has been fixed at seven, but depending upon the local situation, they may be reduced to three. The Church wishes to offer us a panoramic view of the whole trajectory of salvation history, starting with creation, passing through the election and the liberation of Israel to the testimony of the prophets by which this entire history is directed ever more clearly toward Jesus Christ. In the liturgical tradition all these readings were called prophecies. Even when they are not directly foretelling future events, they have a prophetic character, they show us the inner foundation and orientation of history. They cause creation and history to become transparent to what is essential. In this way they take us by the hand and lead us toward Christ, they show us the true Light.

At the Easter Vigil, the journey along the paths of sacred scripture begins with the account of creation. This is the liturgy's way of telling us that the creation story is itself a prophecy. It is not information about the external processes by which the cosmos and man himself came into being. The Fathers of the Church were well aware of this. They did not interpret the story as an account of the process of the origins of things, but rather as a pointer toward the essential, toward the true beginning and end of our being. Now, one might ask: is it really important to speak also of creation during the Easter Vigil? Could we not begin with the events in which God calls man, forms a people for himself, and creates his history with men upon the earth? The answer has to be: no. To omit the creation would be to misunderstand the very history of God with men, to diminish it, to lose sight of its true order of greatness. The sweep of history established by God reaches back to the origins, back to creation. Our profession of faith begins with the words: "We believe in God, the Father Almighty, Creator of heaven and earth." If we omit the beginning of the Credo, the whole history of salvation becomes too limited and too small. The Church is not some kind of association that concerns itself with man's religious needs but is limited to that objective. No, she brings man into contact with God and thus with the source of all things. Therefore we relate to God as Creator, and so we have a responsibility for creation. Our responsibility extends as far as creation because it comes from the Creator. Only because God created everything can he give us life and direct our lives. Life in the Church's faith involves more than a set of feelings and sentiments and perhaps moral obligations. It embraces man in his entirety, from his origins to his eternal destiny. Only because creation belongs to God can we place ourselves completely in his hands. And only because he is the Creator can he give us life forever. Joy over creation, thanksgiving for creation, and responsibility for it all belong together.

The central message of the creation account can be defined more precisely still. In the opening words of his Gospel, St. John sums up the essential meaning of that account in this single statement: "In the beginning was the Word." In effect, the creation account that we listened to earlier is characterized by the regularly recurring phrase: "And God said." The world is a product of the Word, of the *Logos*, as St. John expresses it, using a key term from the Greek language. *"Logos"* means "reason," "sense," "word." It is not reason pure and simple, but creative Reason, that speaks and communicates itself. It is Reason that both is and creates sense. The creation account tells us, then, that the world is a product of creative Reason. Hence it tells us that, far from there being an absence of reason and freedom at the origin of all things, the source of everything is creative Reason, love, and freedom. Here we are faced with the ultimate alternative that is at stake in the dispute between faith and unbelief: are irrationality, lack of freedom, and pure chance the origin of everything, or are reason, freedom, and love at the origin of being? Does the primacy belong to unreason or to reason? This is what everything hinges upon in the final analysis. As believers we answer, with the creation account and with St. John, that in the beginning is reason. In the beginning is freedom. Hence it is good to be a human person. It is not the case that in the expanding universe, at a late stage, in some tiny corner of the cosmos, there evolved randomly some species of living being capable of reasoning and of trying to find rationality within creation, or to bring rationality into it. If man were merely a random product of evolution in some place on the margins of the universe, then his life would make no sense or might even be a chance of nature. But no, Reason is there at the beginning: creative, divine Reason. And because it is Reason, it also created freedom; and because freedom can be abused, there also exist forces harmful to creation. Hence a thick black line, so to speak, has been drawn across the structure of the universe and across the nature of man. But despite this contradiction, creation itself remains good, life remains good, because at the beginning is good Reason, God's creative love. Hence the world can be saved. Hence we can and must place ourselves on the side of reason, freedom, and love—on the side of God who loves us so much that he suffered for us, that from his death there might emerge a new, definitive, and healed life.

The Old Testament account of creation that we listened to clearly indicates this order of realities. But it leads us a further step forward. It has structured the process of creation within the framework of a week leading up to the Sabbath, in which it finds its completion. For Israel, the Sabbath was the day on which all could participate in God's rest, in which man and animal, master and slave, great and small were united in God's freedom. Thus the Sabbath was an expression of the covenant between God and man and creation. In this way, communion between God and man does not appear as something extra, something added later to a world already fully created. The covenant, communion between God and man, is inbuilt at the deepest level of creation. Yes, the covenant is the inner ground of creation, just as creation is the external presupposition of the covenant. God made the world so that there could be a space where he might communicate his love, and from which the response of love might come back to him. From God's perspective, the heart of the man who responds to him is greater and more important than the whole immense material cosmos, for all that the latter allows us to glimpse something of God's grandeur.

Easter and the paschal experience of Christians, however, now require us to take a further step. The Sabbath is the seventh day of the week. After six days in which man in some sense participates in God's work of creation, the Sabbath is the day of rest. But something quite unprecedented happened in the nascent Church: the place of the Sabbath, the seventh day, was taken by the first day. As the day of the liturgical assembly, it is the day for encounter with God through Jesus Christ who as the Risen Lord encountered his followers on the first day, Sunday, after they had found the tomb empty. The structure of the week is overturned. No longer does it point toward the seventh day, as the time to participate in God's rest. It sets out from the first day as the day of encounter with the Risen Lord. This encounter happens afresh at every celebration of the Eucharist, when the Lord enters anew into the midst of his disciples and gives himself to them, allows himself, so to speak, to be touched by them, sits down at table with them. This change is utterly extraordinary, considering that the Sabbath, the seventh day seen as the day of encounter with God, is so profoundly rooted in the Old Testament. If we also bear in mind how much the movement from work toward the rest-day corresponds to a natural rhythm, the dramatic nature of this change is even more striking. This revolutionary development that occurred at the very the beginning of the Church's history can be explained only by the fact that something utterly new happened that day. The first day of the week was the third day after Jesus' death. It was the day when he showed himself to his disciples as the Risen Lord. In truth, this encounter had something unsettling about it. The world had changed. This man who had died was now living with a life that was no longer threatened by any death. A new form of life had been inaugurated, a new dimension of creation. The first day, according to the Genesis account, is the day on which creation begins. Now it was the day of creation in a new way, it had become the day of the new creation. We celebrate the first day. And in so doing we celebrate God the Creator and his creation. Yes, we believe in God, the Creator of heaven and earth. And we celebrate the God who was made man, who suffered, died, was buried, and rose again. We celebrate the definitive victory of the Creator and of his creation. We celebrate this day as the origin and the goal of our existence. We celebrate it because now, thanks to the Risen Lord, it is definitively established that reason is stronger than unreason, truth stronger than lies, love stronger than death. We celebrate the first day because we know that the black line drawn across creation does not last forever. We celebrate it because we know that those words from the end of the creation account have now been definitively fulfilled: "God saw everything that he had made, and behold, it was very good" (Gn 1:31).

## The Earth Seen from Space Is Beautiful and Fragile

From Satellite Connection with the
Crew of the International Space Station (ISS),
May 21, 2011

### SECOND QUESTION

One of the themes I often return to in my discourses concerns the responsibility we all have toward the future of our planet. I recall the serious risks facing the environment and the survival of future generations. Scientists tell us we have to be careful and from an ethical point of view we must develop our consciences as well.

From your extraordinary observation point, how do you see the situation on Earth?

Do you see signs or phenomena to which we need to be more attentive?

Ron Garan, U.S.A.:

Well, Your Holiness, it's a great honor to speak with you and you're right: it really is an extraordinary vantage point we have up here. On the one hand, we can see how indescribably beautiful the planet that we have been given is; but on the other hand, we can really clearly see how fragile it is. Just the atmosphere, for instance: the atmosphere when viewed from space is paper-thin, and to think that this paper-thin layer is all that separates every living thing from the vacuum of space and is all that protects us, is really a sobering thought. You know, it seems to us that it's just incredible to view the earth hanging in the blackness of space and to think that we are all on this together, riding through this beautiful fragile oasis through the universe, it really fills us with a lot of hope to think that all of us on board this incredible orbiting space station that was built by the many nations of our international partnership, to accomplish this tremendous feat in orbit, I think... you know, that just shows that by working together and by cooperating we can overcome many of the problems that face our planet, we could solve many of the challenges that face the inhabitants of our planet.... It really is a wonderful place to live and work, and it's a wonderful place to view our beautiful earth.

## Human Ecology Is an Imperative Need

From Address to Six New Ambassadors Accredited
to the Holy See, June 9, 2011

Since I have the opportunity for a special meeting with each one of you, I would now like to speak more broadly. The first six months of this year have been marked by innumerable tragedies which have concerned nature, technology, and peoples. The magnitude of these catastrophes calls us to wonder. Man comes first, as it is right to remember. Man, to whom God entrusted the good stewardship of nature, cannot be dominated by technology or subjected to it. An awareness of this must bring states to reflect together on the future of the planet in the short term, facing their responsibility for our life and for technology. A human ecology is an imperative need. One of our political and economic priorities must be to adopt in every way a manner of life that respects the environment and supports the research in and use of forms of energy that preserve the patrimony of creation and are safe for human beings. In this regard, it is necessary to review our entire approach to nature. It is not a place solely for exploitation or for play. It is man's native land, in a certain sense his "home." This is fundamental for us. The shift of mentality in this domain, that is, the constraints it brings, allows us rapidly to become more proficient in the art of living together that respects the alliance between man and nature, without which the human family risks disappearing.

Serious reflection must therefore be undertaken and precise and viable solutions proposed. Every government must be committed to protecting nature and to helping it carry out its essential role in humanity's survival. The United Nations seems to me the natural setting for such reflection which, if it is to give priority to solidarity rather than to personal interest, must not be clouded by political and economic interests that are blind and partisan.

It is also right to question oneself about the proper place for technology. Its marvelous potential goes hand in hand with social and ecological disasters. By extending the relational aspect of work to the planet, technology impresses on globalization a particularly accelerated rhythm. Now, it is the human worker who is responsible for this dynamic of progress and not technology which is only a human creation. To stake everything on technology or to believe that it is the exclusive agent for happiness brings a reification of the human being which results in blindness and unhappiness when powers it does not possess are attributed and delegated to it.

It suffices to note the "damage" of progress and the risks to humanity of an all-powerful technology which, ultimately, has not been mastered. Technology that dominates human beings deprives them of their humanity. The pride it engenders has brought an inflexible economic focus into our societies and a certain hedonism that determines behavior subjectively and egotistically.

The weakening of the primacy of the human being brings existential bewilderment and a loss of the meaning of life. For a vision of the human person and of things without a reference to transcendence uproots man from the earth and fundamentally impoverishes his very identity. Hence it is urgently necessary to succeed in combining technology with a strong ethical dimension, for the human capacity to transform and, in a sense, to create the world through his own work is always based on the first and original gift of things that are made by God.[60] Technology must help nature blossom according to the will of the Creator. Working in this way the researcher and the scientist adhere to the design of God, who willed that man be the summit and steward of creation. Solutions with this as its foundation will protect human life and human vulnerability, as well as the rights of present generations and those to come. And humanity will be able to continue to benefit from the progress that man, with his intelligence, succeeds in achieving.

Aware of the risk humanity runs in the face of a technology seen as a more efficient "response" than political voluntarism or the patient effort of education in cultivating morals, government leaders must promote a humanism respectful of the human being's spiritual and religious dimension—because the dignity of the human person does not vary with the fluctuation of opinions. Respecting the human aspiration to justice and peace makes it possible to build a society that promotes itself, when, for example, it supports families or rejects the exclusive primacy of money. A country thrives on the fullness of the life of its citizens, each aware of his or her own responsibilities and each able to bring to bear his or her own convictions.

Furthermore, the natural tendency toward the true and the good is a source of dynamism which generates the desire to collaborate in order to realize the common good. Therefore social

60. Cf. John Paul II, *Centesimus Annus,* n. 37.

life can be constantly enriched by integrating cultural and religious diversity through the sharing of values, a source of brotherhood and communion. Life in society must be considered first and foremost as a spiritual reality. It is the role of political leaders to guide people toward human harmony and toward the wisdom so longed for which must culminate in religious freedom, the authentic face of peace.

## The Created World Is Not Merely a Scenario into Which God's Saving Action Is Inserted, but Rather the Very Beginning of That Marvelous Action

From General Audience, October 19, 2011

### THE GREAT HALLEL (PSALM 136 [135])

Today I would like to meditate with you on a psalm that sums up the entire history of salvation recorded in the Old Testament. It is a great hymn of praise that celebrates the Lord in the multiple, repeated expressions of his goodness throughout human history: it is Psalm 136 or 135 according to the Greco-Latin tradition.

A solemn prayer of thanksgiving, known as the "Great Hallel," this psalm is traditionally sung at the end of the Jewish Passover meal and was probably also prayed by Jesus at the Last Supper celebrated with his disciples. In fact, the annotation of the Evangelists, "and when they had sung a hymn, they went out to the Mount of Olives" (cf. Mt 26:30; Mk 14:26), would seem to allude to it.

The horizon of praise thus appears to illumine the difficult path to Golgotha. The whole of Psalm 136 unfolds in the form of a litany, marked by the antiphonal refrain: "for his steadfast love endures forever." The many wonders God has worked in human history and his continuous intervention on behalf of his people are listed in the composition. Furthermore, to every proclamation of the Lord's saving action the antiphon responds with the basic impetus of praise.

The eternal love of God is a love which, in accordance with the Hebrew term used, suggestive of fidelity, mercy, kindness, grace, and tenderness, is the unifying motif of the entire psalm. The refrain always takes the same form, whereas the regular paradigmatic manifestations of God's love change: creation, liberation through the Exodus, the gift of land, the Lord's provident and constant help for his people and for every created being.

After a triple invitation to give thanks to God as sovereign (Ps 136:1–3), the Lord is celebrated as the One who works "great wonders" (Ps 136:4), the first of which is the Creation: the heavens, the earth, the heavenly bodies (Ps 136:5–9). The created world is not merely a scenario into which God's saving action is inserted, rather is the very beginning of that marvelous action. With the creation, the Lord shows himself in all his goodness and beauty, he commits himself to life, revealing a desire for goodness which gives rise to every other action of salvation.

And in our psalm, echoing the first chapter of Genesis, the principal elements of the created world are summed up, with special insistence on the heavenly bodies, the sun, the moon, and the stars, magnificent created things that govern the day and the night. Nothing is said here of the creation of human beings but they are ever present; the sun and the moon are for them—for men and women—so as to structure human time, setting it in relation to the Creator, especially by denoting the liturgical seasons. And it is precisely the Feast of Easter that is immediately evoked, when, passing to God's manifestation of himself in history, the great event of the Exodus, freedom from slavery in Egypt begins, whose most significant elements are outlined.

The liberation from Egypt begins with the plague of killing the Egyptian firstborn, the Exodus from Egypt, the crossing of the Red Sea, the journey through the desert to the entry into the Promised Land (Ps 136:10–20). This is the very first moment of Israel's history; God intervened powerfully to lead his people to freedom; through Moses, his envoy, he asserted himself before Pharaoh, revealing himself in his full grandeur and at last broke down the resistance of the Egyptians with the terrible plague of the death of the firstborn. Israel could thus leave the country of slavery taking with it the gold of its oppressors (cf. Ex 12:35–36) and "defiantly" (Ex 14:8), in the exulting sign of victory.

At the Red Sea too the Lord acted with merciful power. Before an Israel so terrified by the sight of the Egyptians in pursuit as to regret its departure from Egypt (cf. Ex 14:10–12), God, as our psalm says, "divided the Red Sea in sunder ... and made the people of Israel pass through the midst of it ... but overthrew Pharaoh and his host" (Ps 136:13–15). The image of the Red Sea "divided" into two seems to call to mind the idea of the sea as a great monster hacked into two and thereby rendered harmless. The might of the Lord overcomes the danger of the forces of nature and of these soldiers deployed in battle array by men: the sea, which seemed to bar the way of the People of God, let Israel cross on dry ground and then swept over the Egyptians, submerging them. Thus the full salvific force of the Lord's "mighty hand, and an outstretched arm" (cf. Dt 5:15; 7:19; 26:8) was demonstrated: the unjust oppressor was vanquished, engulfed by the waters, while the people of God "walked on dry ground through the sea," continuing its journey to freedom.

Our psalm now refers to this journey, recalling in one short phrase Israel's long pilgrimage toward the promised land: he "led his people through the wilderness, for his steadfast love endures forever" (Ps 136:16). These few words refer to a forty-year experience, a crucial period for Israel which in letting itself be guided by the Lord learned to live in faith, obedience, and docility to God's law. These were difficult years, marked by hardship in the desert, but also happy years, trusting in the Lord with filial trust. It was the time of "youth," as the Prophet Jeremiah describes it in speaking to Israel in the Lord's name with words full of tenderness and nostalgia: "I remember the devotion of your youth, your love as a bride, how you followed me in the wilderness, in a land not sown" (Jer 2:2).

The Lord, like the shepherd of Psalm 23 [22] whom we contemplated in a catechesis, for forty years guided, taught, and cherished his people, leading it right to the promised land, also overcoming the resistance and hostility of enemy peoples that wished to block its way to salvation (cf. Ps 136:17–20).

So as the "great wonders" that our psalm lists unfold, we reach the moment of the conclusive gift, the fulfillment of the divine promise made to the Fathers: "gave their land as a heritage, for his steadfast love endures forever; a heritage to Israel his servant, for his steadfast love endures forever" (Ps 136:21–22).

Then, in celebrating the Lord's eternal love, the gift of land was commemorated, a gift that the people were to receive but without ever taking possession of it, continuing to live in an attitude of grateful acknowledgment and gratitude.

Israel received the land it was to live in as "a heritage," a generic term which designates the possession of a good received from another person, a right of ownership which specifically refers to the paternal patrimony. One of God's prerogatives is "giving"; and now, at the end of the journey of the Exodus, Israel, the recipient of the gift, enters as a son or daughter the land of the promise now fulfilled. The time of wandering, of living in tents, of living a precarious life, is over.

It was then that the happy period of permanence began, of joy in building houses, of planting vineyards, of living in security (cf. Dt 8:7–13). Yet it was also the time of the temptation to idolatry, contamination with pagans, self-sufficiency that led to the Origin of the gift being forgotten.

Accordingly, the psalmist mentions Israel's low estate and foes, a reality of death in which the Lord, once again, reveals himself as Savior: "He... remembered us in our low estate, for his steadfast love endures forever; and rescued us from our foes, for his steadfast love endures forever" (Ps 136:23–24).

At this point a question arises: how can we make this psalm our own prayer, how can we ourselves claim this psalm as our own prayer? What is important is the psalm's setting, for at the beginning and at the end is the creation. Let us return to this point: the creation as God's great gift by which we live and in which he reveals himself in his great goodness. Therefore, to think of the creation as a gift of God is a common point for all of us.

The history of salvation then follows. We can of course say: this liberation from Egypt, the time in the desert, the entry into the Holy Land, and all the other subsequent problems are very remote from us, they are not part of our own history. Yet we must be attentive to the fundamental structure of this prayer. The basic structure is that Israel remembers the Lord's goodness. In this history dark valleys, arduous journeys, and death succeed one another but Israel recalls that God was good and can survive in this dark valley, in this valley of death, because it remembers. It remembers the Lord's goodness and his power; his mercy is effective forever. And this is also important for us: to remember the Lord's goodness. Memory strongly sustains hope. Memory tells us: God exists, God is good, his mercy endures forever. So it is that memory unfolds, even in the darkest day or time, showing the way toward the future. It represents "great lights" and is our guiding star. We too have good memories of the goodness, of God's merciful love that endures forever.

Israel's history is a former memory for us, too, of how God revealed himself, how he created a people of his own. Then God became man, one of us: he lived with us, he suffered with us, he died for us. He stays with us in the Sacrament and in the Word. It is a history, a memory of God's goodness that assures us of his goodness: his love endures forever. And then, in these two thousand years of the Church's history there is always, again and again, the Lord's goodness. After the dark period of the Nazi and Communist persecution, God set us free, he showed that he is good, that he is powerful, that his mercy endures forever. And, as in our common, collective history, this memory of God's goodness is present, it helps us and becomes for us a star of hope so that each one also has his or her personal story of salvation.

We must truly treasure this story, and in order to trust must keep ever present in our mind the memory of the great things he has also worked in my life: his mercy endures forever. And if today I am immersed in the dark night, tomorrow he sets me free, for his mercy is eternal.

Let us return to the psalm, because at the end it returns to the creation. The Lord, it says, "gives food to all flesh, for his steadfast love endures forever" (Ps 136:25). The prayer of the psalm concludes with an invitation to praise: "Give thanks to the God of heaven, for his steadfast love endures forever".

The Lord is our good and provident Father, who gives his children their heritage and lavishes life-giving food upon all. God who created the heavens and the earth and the great heavenly bodies, who entered human history to bring all his children to salvation is the God who fills the universe with his presence of goodness, caring for life and providing bread.

The invisible power of the Creator and Lord of which the psalm sings is revealed in the humble sign of the bread he gives us, with which he enables us to live. And so it is that this daily bread symbolizes and sums up the love of God as Father and opens us to the fulfillment of the New Testament, to that "Bread of Life," the Eucharist, which accompanies us in our lives as believers, anticipating the definitive joy of the messianic banquet in heaven.

Brothers and sisters, the praise and blessing of Psalm 136 [135], has made us review the most important stages in the history of salvation, to reach the Paschal Mystery in which God's saving action reaches its culmination. Let us therefore celebrate with grateful joy the Creator, Savior, and faithful Father, who "so loved the world that he gave his only Son, that whoever believes in him should not perish but have eternal life" (Jn 3:16). In the fullness of time, the Son of God became man to give life, for the salvation of each one of us, and gave himself as bread in the Eucharistic mystery to enable us to enter his covenant which makes us his children. May both God's merciful goodness and his sublime "steadfast love forever" reach far afield.

I would therefore like to conclude this catechesis by making my own the words that St. John wrote in his First Letter and that we must always have in mind in our prayers: "See what love the Father has given us, that we should be called children of God; and so we are" (1 Jn 3:1).

## Be Praised My Lord through All Your Creatures

From Address to Students Participating in a
Meeting Promoted by the Sister Nature
Foundation, November 28, 2011

I welcome you with great joy at this meeting dedicated to your commitment to "Sister Nature," to use the name of the Foundation that has sponsored it. I cordially greet Cardinal Rodríguez Maradiaga and thank him for his words to me also on your behalf, and for his gift of the precious facsimile of Codex 338 which contains the most ancient Franciscan sources.

I greet the president, Mr. Roberto Leoni, as well as the authorities and important figures present and the numerous teachers and parents. However, above all I greet you, dear boys and girls, dear young people! It is precisely you I wanted to meet, and I would like to tell you that I deeply appreciate your decision to be "guardians of creation" and that you have my full support in this.

First of all we must remember that your foundation and this meeting itself have a profoundly Franciscan inspiration. Besides, today's date was chosen to commemorate the proclamation of St. Francis of Assisi as patron of ecology by my beloved predecessor, John Paul II, in 1979. You all know that St. Francis is also patron of Italy. However, you may not know that it was Pope Pius XII who declared him such in 1939, when he described him as "the most Italian of saints and the saintliest of Italians."

Thus if the patron saint of Italy is also the patron of ecology, it seems right to me that young people and young Italians should have a special feeling for "Sister Nature" and busy themselves in actively defending her.

Indeed when one studies Italian literature one of the first texts found in the anthologies is the "Canticle of Brother Sun" or "of the Creatures" by St. Francis of Assisi: *"Altissimo, onnipotente, bon Signore!"* (Most high, all powerful, all good Lord). This canticle sheds light on the proper place to give the Creator, the One who called the whole great symphony of creatures into existence: *"Tue so' le laude, la gloria e l'honore et onne benedictione. . . . Laudato sie, mi' Signore, cum tucte le Tue creature"* (All praise is yours, all glory, all honor, and all blessings. . . . Be praised, my Lord, through all your creatures).

These verses rightly belong to your cultural and scholastic tradition. However, they are first and foremost a prayer that teaches the heart dialogue with God, teaches it to see in every created being the impression of the great heavenly Artist, as we also read in the most beautiful Psalm 19 [18]: "The heavens are telling the glory of God; and the firmament proclaims his handiwork.... There is no speech, nor are there words; their voice is not heard; yet their voice goes out through all the earth" (vv. 1:4–5).

Friar Francis, faithful to sacred scripture, invites us to recognize nature as a stupendous book, that speaks to us of God, of his beauty and of his goodness. Only think that the "Poverello" of Assisi always asked the friar of the convent in charge of the vegetable garden not to grow vegetables on all the land but to leave part of it for flowers, indeed to tend a beautiful flowerbed full of flowers so that passersby might raise their thoughts to God, the Creator of so many beautiful things.[61]

Dear friends, while the Church admires the most important scientific research and discoveries, she has never ceased to remember that in respecting the Creator's impression on the whole of creation, we understand better our true and deep human identity. If it is lived well, this respect can also help young men and women discover their personal talents and approaches and hence train for a specific profession which they will always seek to carry out with respect for the environment.

If, in fact, man forgets in his work that he is a collaborator of God, he can do violence to creation and cause untold damage that always has negative consequences, also on human beings, as we have unfortunately seen on various occasions.

61. Tommaso da Celano, *St. Francis of Assisi* (London: J. M. Dent, 1908), 24:53.

Today, more than ever, it appears clear to us that respect for the environment cannot fail to recognize the value and inviolability of the human person in every phase of life and in every condition. Respect for the human being and respect for nature are one and the same, but they will both be able to develop and to reach their full dimension if we respect the Creator and his creature in the human being and in nature. In this regard, dear young people, I am certain that you are my allies, true "custodians of life and of Creation."

I would now like to take this opportunity also to address a special word to the teachers and to the authorities present here. I would like to emphasize the great importance of education in this field of ecology too. I gladly agreed with the suggestion to hold this meeting because it involves such a large number of very young students and because it has a clear educational perspective. In fact, it is obvious by now that there will be no good future for humanity on earth unless we teach everyone a lifestyle that is more responsible toward creation.

And I underscore the importance of the word "creation" because the great and marvelous tree of life is not the fruit of a blind and irrational evolution. Rather, this evolution reflects the creative will of the Creator and his beauty and goodness. This style of responsibility is learned first of all at home and at school. I therefore encourage parents, heads of schools, and teachers to undertake to pay constant educational and didactic attention to this aim. In addition, it is indispensable that the proper institutions—which are well represented here today—support families and schools in this endeavor.

Dear friends, let us entrust these thoughts and aspirations to the Virgin Mary, Mother of all humanity. As we have just begun the season of Advent, she accompanies and guides us to recognize Christ as the center of the cosmos, the light that illumines every person and every creature. St. Francis, moreover, teaches us to sing, with all creation, a hymn of praise and thanksgiving to the heavenly Father, Giver of every gift. I warmly thank you for coming in such large numbers and I gladly accompany you with my blessing in your studies, your work, and your commitment.

I spoke of singing, let us sing the Our Father together, the great prayer that Jesus taught us all.

PART 2

# THE ENVIRONMENT, SCIENCE, AND TECHNOLOGY

## The Harmony of Faith and Knowledge

From Meeting with the Youth of Rome and the Lazio Region in
Preparation for the Twenty-first World Youth Day, April 6, 2006

Holy Father, I am Giovanni, I am seventeen years old, I am studying at Giovanni Giorgi technological and scientific secondary school in Rome, and I belong to Holy Mary Mother of Mercy Parish.

I ask you to help us to understand better how biblical revelation and scientific theory can converge in the search for truth.

We are often led to believe that knowledge and faith are each other's enemies; that knowledge and technology are the same thing; that it was through mathematical logic that everything was discovered; that the world is the result of an accident; and that if mathematics did not discover the theorem God, it is because God simply does not exist.

In short, especially when we are studying, it is not always easy to trace everything back to a divine plan inherent in the nature and history of human beings. Thus, faith at times vacillates or is reduced to a simple sentimental act.

Holy Father, like all young people, I too am thirsting for the truth: but what can I do to harmonize knowledge and faith?

The great Galileo said that God wrote the book of nature in the form of the language of mathematics. He was convinced that God has given us two books: the book of sacred scripture and the book of nature. And the language of nature—this was his conviction—is mathematics, so it is a language of God, a language of the Creator.

Let us now reflect on what mathematics is: in itself, it is an abstract system, an invention of the human spirit which as such in its purity does not exist. It is always approximated, but as such is an intellectual system, a great, ingenious invention of the human spirit.

The surprising thing is that this invention of our human intellect is truly the key to understanding nature, that nature is truly structured in a mathematical way, and that our mathematics, invented by our human mind, is truly the instrument for working with nature, to put it at our service, to use it through technology.

It seems to me almost incredible that an invention of the human mind and the structure of the universe coincide. Mathematics, which we invented, really gives us access to the nature of the universe and makes it possible for us to use it.

Therefore, the intellectual structure of the human subject and the objective structure of reality coincide: the subjective reason and the objective reason of nature are identical. I think that this coincidence between what we thought up and how nature is fulfilled and behaves is a great enigma and a great challenge, for we see that, in the end, it is "one" reason that links them both.

Our reason could not discover this other reason were there not an identical antecedent reason for both.

In this sense it really seems to me that mathematics—in which as such God cannot appear—shows us the intelligent structure of the universe. Now, there are also theories of chaos, but they are limited because if chaos had the upper hand, all technology would become impossible. Only because our mathematics is reliable, is technology reliable.

Our knowledge, which is at last making it possible to work with the energies of nature, supposes the reliable and intelligent structure of matter. Thus, we see that there is a subjective rationality and an objectified rationality in matter which coincide.

Of course, no one can now prove—as is proven in an experiment, in technical laws—that they both really originated in a single intelligence, but it seems to me that this unity of intelligence, behind the two intelligences, really appears in our world. And the more we can delve into the world with our intelligence, the more clearly the plan of creation appears.

In the end, to reach the definitive question I would say: God exists or he does not exist. There are only two options. Either one recognizes the priority of reason, of creative Reason that is at the beginning of all things and is the principle of all things—the priority of reason is also the priority of freedom—or one holds the priority of the irrational, inasmuch as everything that functions on our earth and in our lives would be only accidental, marginal, an irrational result—reason would be a product of irrationality.

One cannot ultimately "prove" either project, but the great option of Christianity is the option for rationality and for the priority of reason. This seems to me to be an excellent option, which shows us that behind everything is a great Intelligence to which we can entrust ourselves. However, the true problem challenging faith today seems to me to be the evil in the world: we ask ourselves how it can be compatible with the Creator's rationality. And here we truly need God, who was made flesh and shows us that he is not only a mathematical reason but that this original Reason is also love. If we look at the great options, the

Christian option today is the one that is the most rational and the most human.

Therefore, we can confidently work out a philosophy, a vision of the world based on this priority of reason, on this trust that the creating Reason is love and that this love is God.

## Remembrance of the Twentieth Anniversary of the Tragedy at Chernobyl

From General Audience, April 26, 2006

Today is the twentieth anniversary of the tragic accident which occurred in the nuclear power plant of Chernobyl. I feel the need to express my great appreciation for the families, associations, civil authorities, and Christian communities who, over these years, have striven to house and care for the people, especially the children, struck by the consequences of that painful event. As once again we pray for the victims of so immense a tragedy and for those who carry the signs on their bodies, we call on the Lord to enlighten the people responsible for the fate of humanity that they, through joint efforts, put all their energies at the service of peace, while respecting the needs of mankind and of nature.

## Environment, Human Person, Spiritual Values: Three Challenges to Face in the Service of Justice Inspired by Charity

From Letter to Professor Mary Ann Glendon, President of the
Pontifical Academy of Social Sciences, on the Occasion of the
Thirteenth Plenary Session, April 28, 2007

As the Pontifical Academy of Social Sciences gathers for its thirteenth plenary session, I am pleased to greet you and your distinguished confreres and to convey my prayerful good wishes for your deliberations.

The academy's meeting this year is devoted to an examination of the theme: "Charity and Justice in the Relations among Peoples and Nations." The Church cannot fail to be interested in this subject, inasmuch as the pursuit of justice and the promotion of the civilization of love are essential aspects of her mission of proclaiming the Gospel of Jesus Christ. Certainly the building of a just society is the primary responsibility of the political order, both in individual states and in the international community. As such, it demands, at every level, a disciplined exercise of practical reason and a training of the will in order to discern and achieve the specific requirements of justice in full respect for the common good and the inalienable dignity of each individual. In my encyclical *Deus Caritas Est,* I wished to reaffirm, at the beginning of my pontificate, the Church's desire to contribute to this necessary purification of reason, to help form consciences and to stimulate a greater response to the genuine requirements of justice. At the same time, I wished to

95

emphasize that, even in the most just society, there will always be a place for charity: "there is no ordering of the state so just that it can eliminate the need for a service of love."[1]

The Church's conviction of the inseparability of justice and charity is ultimately born of her experience of the revelation of God's infinite justice and mercy in Jesus Christ, and it finds expression in her insistence that man himself and his irreducible dignity must be at the center of political and social life. Her teaching, which is addressed not only to believers but to all people of good will, thus appeals to right reason and a sound understanding of human nature in proposing principles capable of guiding individuals and communities in the pursuit of a social order marked by justice, freedom, fraternal solidarity, and peace. At the heart of that teaching, as you well know, is the principle of the universal destination of all the goods of creation. According to this fundamental principle, everything that the earth produces and all that man transforms and manufactures, all his knowledge and technology, is meant to serve the material and spiritual development and fulfillment of the human family and all its members.

From this integrally human perspective we can understand more fully the essential role which charity plays in the pursuit of justice. My predecessor, Pope John Paul II, was convinced that justice alone is insufficient to establish truly humane and fraternal relations within society. "In every sphere of interpersonal relationships," he maintained, "justice must, so to speak, be 'corrected' to a considerable extent by that love which, as St. Paul proclaims, 'is patient and kind' or, in other words, possess-

1. Benedict XVI, *Deus Caritas Est*, n. 28.

96

es the characteristics of that merciful love which is so much of the essence of the Gospel and Christianity."[2] Charity, in a word, not only enables justice to become more inventive and to meet new challenges; it also inspires and purifies humanity's efforts to achieve authentic justice and thus the building of a society worthy of man.

At a time when "concern for our neighbor transcends the confines of national communities and has increasingly broadened its horizon to the whole world," the intrinsic relationship between charity and justice needs to be more clearly understood and emphasized.[3] In expressing my confidence that your discussions in these days will prove fruitful in this regard, I would like briefly to direct your attention to three specific challenges facing our world, challenges which I believe can only be met through a firm commitment to that greater justice which is inspired by charity.

The first concerns the environment and sustainable development. The international community recognizes that the world's resources are limited and that it is the duty of all peoples to implement policies to protect the environment in order to prevent the destruction of that natural capital whose fruits are necessary for the well-being of humanity. To meet this challenge, what is required is an interdisciplinary approach such as you have employed. Also needed is a capacity to assess and forecast, to monitor the dynamics of environmental change and sustainable growth, and to draw up and apply solutions at an international level. Particular attention must be paid to the fact

2. John Paul II, Encyclical Letter *Dives in Misericordia* (November 30, 1980), n. 14.
3. Benedict XVI, *Deus Caritas Est,* n. 30.

that the poorest countries are likely to pay the heaviest price for ecological deterioration. In my Message for the 2007 World Day of Peace, I pointed out that "the destruction of the environment, its improper or selfish use, and the violent hoarding of the earth's resources... are the consequences of an inhumane concept of development. Indeed, if development were limited to the technical-economic aspect, obscuring the moral-religious dimension, it would not be an integral human development, but a one-sided distortion which would end up by unleashing man's destructive capacities."[4] In meeting the challenges of environmental protection and sustainable development, we are called to promote and "safeguard the moral conditions for an authentic 'human ecology.'"[5] This in turn calls for a responsible relationship not only with creation but also with our neighbors, near and far, in space and time, and with the Creator.

## The Irresponsible Exploitation of the Environment Reflects an Inhumane Concept of Development

From Address to His Excellency Mr. Stefán Lárus Stefánsson,
New Ambassador of Iceland to the Holy See, June 1, 2007

The Church's diplomatic relations form a part of her mission of service to the international community. This engagement with civil society is anchored in her conviction that the hope of building a more just world must acknowledge man's super-

4. Benedict XVI, Message for the 2007 World Day of Peace, n. 9, January 1, 2007.
5. John Paul II, Encyclical Letter *Centesimus Annus* (May 1, 1991), n. 38.

natural vocation. It is from God that men and women receive their essential dignity and with it the capacity and the call to direct their steps toward truth and goodness.[6] Within this broad perspective we can counter the pragmatic tendency, so prevalent today, which tends to engage only with the symptoms of social fragmentation and moral confusion. Where humanity's transcendent dimension is brought to light, individuals' hearts and minds are drawn to God and to the very essence of human life—truth, beauty, moral values, other persons, and being itself[7]—leading them to a sure foundation and vision of hope for society.

As Your Excellency has observed, integral to Iceland's history is the Gospel of Jesus Christ including its missionary dimension. For over a thousand years Christianity has shaped Icelandic culture. In more recent times these spiritual roots have found a degree of resonance in your relations with Europe. This common cultural and moral identity, forged by the universal values of Christianity, is not simply of historical importance. Being foundational, it can remain as a "ferment" of civilization. In this regard, I commend your government's open recognition of Christianity's fundamental role in the life of your nation. When public moral discernment is not emptied of meaning by a secularism which neglects truth while highlighting mere opinion, both civil and religious leaders can uphold the absolute values and ideals inherent in the dignity of every person. In this way together they can offer our young people a future of happiness and fulfillment.

6. Cf. John Paul II, Encyclical Letter *Fides et Ratio* (September 14, 1998), n. 5.
7. Cf. ibid., n. 83.

Iceland's significant contribution to the security and social development of the worldwide human family belies its size and the number of its citizens. Your nation's commitment to supporting peace-keeping operations and aid projects is readily recognized by the Holy See and esteemed by the international community. While your founder-member status of NATO and your long history of United Nations Organization membership are well known, perhaps less known is the highly effective work of the Icelandic Crisis Response Unit. This well-respected service is an outstanding example, from the field of international relations, of men and women enlightened by the splendor of truth, setting out on the path of peace.[8] Such initiatives aptly illustrate how the will to resolve conflicts peacefully and the determination to govern by justice, integrity, and service of the common good can be achieved.

Preservation of the environment and promotion of sustainable development are increasingly seen as matters of grave concern for all. As reflections and studies on ecology mature, it becomes more and more evident that there is an inseparable link between peace with creation, and peace among people. The full understanding of this relationship is found in the natural and moral order with which God has created man and has endowed the earth.[9]

The close connection between these two ecologies comes into sharp focus when the questions of food resources and energy supply are addressed. The international community recog-

8. Cf. Benedict XVI, Message for the 2006 World Day of Peace, n. 3, January 1, 2006.

9. Cf. Benedict XVI, Message for the 2007 World Day of Peace, nn. 8–9, January 1, 2007.

nizes that the world's resources are limited. Yet the duty to implement policies to prevent the destruction of that natural capital is not always observed. Any irresponsible exploitation of the environment or hoarding of land or marine resources reflects an inhumane concept of development, the consequences of which affect the poorest countries most. Iceland, acutely aware of these matters, has rightly emphasized the relationship between the Millennium Development Goals and environment protection and the sustainable use of resources, and has laudably drawn attention to the fact that the large majority of those who make their living from fisheries are families in the developing world.

Mr. Ambassador, the members of the Catholic Church in your country, though few, reach out to the entire Icelandic society. Expressing the Church's belief in the "unbreakable bond between love of God and love of neighbor,"[10] they undertake works of charity from their small but vibrant parish communities. A particularly beautiful example of this is found in the Carmelite convent of contemplative life in Hafnarfjordur, where the sisters pray daily for the needs of all Icelanders.

Your Excellency, I am confident that the mission which you begin today will help to strengthen even further the cordial bonds of understanding and cooperation between Iceland and the Holy See. Please rest assured that the various offices of the Roman Curia are ready to assist you in the fulfillment of your duties. Upon you, your family, and your fellow citizens I invoke the abundant blessings of Almighty God.

10. Benedict XVI, *Deus Caritas Est*, n. 16.

## Scientific Knowledge and Technology Are Always Applied in Full Respect for International Rights

From Angelus, Castel Gandolfo, July 29, 2007

Last Sunday, recalling the "Note" that Pope Benedict XV addressed to the belligerent countries in the First World War on 1 August ninety years ago, I dwelled on the theme of peace.

Now a new occasion invites me to reflect on another important subject connected with this theme. Precisely today, in fact, is the fiftieth anniversary of the establishment of the charter of the IAEA, the International Atomic Energy Agency, instituted with the mandate to "accelerate and enlarge the contribution of atomic energy to peace, health, and prosperity throughout the world."[11]

The Holy See, fully approving the goals of this organization, is a member of it since its founding, and continues to support its activity.

The epochal changes that have occurred in the last fifty years demonstrate how, in the difficult crossroads in which humanity finds itself, the commitment to encourage non-proliferation of nuclear arms, to promote a progressive and agreed-upon nuclear disarmament, and to support the use of peaceful and safe nuclear technology for authentic development, respecting the environment and ever mindful of the most disadvantaged populations, is always more present and urgent.

11. International Atomic Energy Agency, *The Statute of the IAEA*, art. 2.

I therefore hope that the efforts of those who work with determination to bring about these three objectives may be achieved, with the goal that "[t]he resources which would be saved could then be employed in projects of development capable of benefiting all their people, especially the poor."[12] It is also good on this occasion to repeat how: "In place of... the arms race, there must be substituted a common effort to mobilize resources toward objectives of moral, cultural and economic development, 'redefining the priorities and hierarchies of values.'"[13] Again we entrust to the intercession of Mary Most Holy our prayer for peace, in particular so that scientific knowledge and technology are always applied with a sense of responsibility and for the common good, in full respect for international rights.

Let us pray so that men live in peace and that they may be as brothers, sons of one Father: God.

## *Strengthening the Alliance between Man and the Environment*

From Angelus, Castel Gandolfo, September 16, 2007

Today is the twentieth anniversary of the adoption of the Montreal Protocol on substances that impoverish the ozone layer, causing serious damage to the human being and the ecosystem.

In the past two decades, thanks to exemplary collaboration in the international community between politics, science, and

---

12. Benedict XVI, Message for the 2006 World Day of Peace, n. 13, January 1, 2006.
13. *Catechism of the Catholic Church* (1993), n. 2438.

economics, important results have been achieved with positive repercussions on the present and future generations.

I hope that cooperation on everyone's part will be intensified in order to promote the common good and the development and safeguard of creation, strengthening the alliance between man and the environment, which must mirror the creative love of God from whom we come and to whom we are bound.

## Family, Human Community, and the Environment

From Message for the Celebration of the
World Day of Peace, January 1, 2008

7. The family needs a home, a fit environment in which to develop its proper relationships. *For the human family, this home is the earth,* the environment that God the Creator has given us to inhabit with creativity and responsibility. We need to care for the environment: it has been entrusted to men and women to be protected and cultivated with responsible freedom, with the good of all as a constant guiding criterion. Human beings, obviously, are of supreme worth vis-à-vis creation as a whole. Respecting the environment does not mean considering material or animal nature more important than man. Rather, it means not selfishly considering nature to be at the complete disposal of our own interests, for future generations also have the right to reap its benefits and to exhibit toward nature the same responsible freedom that we claim for ourselves. Nor must we overlook the poor, who are excluded in many cases from the goods of creation

destined for all. Humanity today is rightly concerned about the ecological balance of tomorrow. It is important for assessments in this regard to be carried out prudently, in dialogue with experts and people of wisdom, uninhibited by ideological pressure to draw hasty conclusions, and above all with the aim of reaching agreement on a model of sustainable development capable of ensuring the well-being of all while respecting environmental balances. If the protection of the environment involves costs, they should be justly distributed, taking due account of the different levels of development of various countries and the need for solidarity with future generations. Prudence does not mean failing to accept responsibilities and postponing decisions; it means being committed to making joint decisions after pondering responsibly the road to be taken, decisions aimed at strengthening that covenant between human beings and the environment, which should mirror the creative love of God, from whom we come and toward whom we are journeying.

8. In this regard, it is essential to "sense" that the earth is "our common home" and, in our stewardship and service to all, to choose the path of dialogue rather than the path of unilateral decisions. Further international agencies may need to be established in order to confront together the stewardship of this "home" of ours; more important, however, is the need for ever greater conviction about the need for responsible cooperation. The problems looming on the horizon are complex and time is short. In order to face this situation effectively, there is a need to act in harmony. One area where there is a particular need to intensify dialogue between nations is that of the *stewardship of the earth's energy resources*. The technologically advanced countries

are facing two pressing needs in this regard: on the one hand, to reassess the high levels of consumption due to the present model of development, and on the other hand to invest sufficient resources in the search for alternative sources of energy and for greater energy efficiency. The emerging countries are hungry for energy, but at times this hunger is met in a way harmful to poor countries which, due to their insufficient infrastructures, including their technological infrastructures, are forced to undersell the energy resources they do possess. At times, their very political freedom is compromised by forms of protectorate or, in any case, by forms of conditioning which appear clearly humiliating.

## New Men for a New World

From Message for the Eighty-second World Mission Sunday
2008, Servants and Apostles of Christ Jesus, May 11, 2008

### HUMANITY IS IN NEED OF LIBERATION

Humanity needs to be liberated and redeemed. Creation itself—as St. Paul says—suffers and nurtures the hope that it will share in the freedom of the children of God (cf. Rom 8:19–22). These words are true in today's world too. Creation is suffering. Creation is suffering and waiting for real freedom; it is waiting for a different, better world; it is waiting for "redemption." And deep down it knows that this new world that is awaited supposes a new man; it supposes "children of God."

Let us take a closer look at the situation of today's world. While, on the one hand, the international panorama presents prospects for promising economic and social development, on the other it brings some great concerns to our attention about the very future of man. Violence, in many cases, marks the relations between persons and peoples. Poverty oppresses millions of inhabitants. Discrimination and sometimes even persecution for racial, cultural, and religious reasons drive many people to flee from their own countries in order to seek refuge and protection elsewhere. Technological progress, when it is not aimed at the dignity and good of man or directed toward solidarity-based development, loses its potentiality as a factor of hope and runs the risk, on the contrary, of increasing already existing imbalances and injustices. There is, moreover, a constant threat regarding the man-environment relation due to the indiscriminate use of resources, with repercussions on the physical and mental health of human beings. Humanity's future is also put at risk by the attempts on his life, which take on various forms and means.

Before this scenario, "buffeted between hope and anxiety... and burdened down with uneasiness,"[14] with concern we ask ourselves: What will become of humanity and creation? Is there hope for the future, or rather, is there a future for humanity? And what will this future be like? The answer to these questions comes to those of us who believe from the Gospel. Christ is our future, and as I wrote in the encyclical letter *Spe Salvi,* his Gospel is a "life-changing" communication that gives hope, throws open the dark door of time, and illuminates the future of humanity and the universe.[15]

---

14. Second Vatican Council, *Gaudium et Spes,* n. 4.
15. Cf. ibid., n. 2.

## Natural Law as a Guarantee against Manipulations and Abuses against Man

From Address to Participants at the Plenary Session
of the International Theological Commission,
December 5, 2008

Then, regarding the third theme, "sense and method of theology," that has been the special object of study in this quinquennial, I am keen to underline its relevance and actuality. In a "planetary society" as that which is being formed today, theologians are asked by the public opinion above all to promote dialogue between religions and cultures, to contribute to the development of an ethic that has as its own base network peace, justice, and the defense of the natural environment. And this truly concerns fundamental goods. But a theology limited to these noble objectives would lose not only its own identity, but the very foundation of these goods. The first priority of theology, as already indicated in its name, is to speak of God, to think of God. And theology speaks of God not as a hypothesis of our thought. It speaks of God because God himself speaks with us. The real work of the theologian is to enter into the Word of God, to seek to understand it for what is possible, and to make it understood to our world, and thus to find the responses to our important questions. In this work it also appears that faith is not only not contrary to reason, but it opens the eyes of reason, it expands our horizons and it permits us to find the responses necessary to the challenges of the various times.

## More Modest Lifestyles to Slow Down
## Environmental Degradation

From Address to Participants at a Meeting Sponsored
by the Youth Tourist Center and the International
Office for Social Tourism, Castel Gandolfo,
September 27, 2008

Our meeting is taking place on the occasion of today's celebration of World Tourism Day. The theme this year—"Tourism Responding to the Challenge of Climate Change"—points to a very timely problem, which concerns the potential of the tourist sector with regard to the state of the planet and of humanity's well-being. Both your institutions seek to promote a tourism attentive to the integral advancement of the person, with a view to sustainability and solidarity. This makes you qualified agents in the work of safeguarding and responsibly making the most of the resources of creation, an immense gift of God to humanity.

Humanity is duty-bound to protect this treasure and to counter the indiscriminate use of the earth's goods. Without an adequate ethical and moral limit, human behavior can in fact become a threat and a challenge. Experience teaches that the responsible management of creation is, or should be, part of a healthy and sustainable tourist economy. On the contrary, the improper use of nature and the abuse inflicted on the culture of local peoples also damage tourism. Learning to respect the environment also teaches respect for others and for oneself. In 1991, in his encyclical *Centesimus Annus,* my beloved predecessor John Paul II had already denounced the excessive and arbitrary consumption of resources, recalling that man is God's collaborator in the work of creation and cannot replace him. He also emphasized that humanity today "must be conscious of its duties and obligations toward future generations."[16]

It is therefore necessary, especially in the context of tourism, a great exploiter of nature, that everyone aim for a balanced management of our habitat, of what is our common home and will be for all who come after us. Environmental degradation can only be slowed down by spreading an appropriate behavioral culture entailing more modest ways of living. Hence the importance, as I recently recalled, of teaching *a responsible code of ethics* and of making "more constructive proposals so as to guarantee the good of future generations."[17]

In addition, the Church shares with your institutions and other similar organizations the commitment to foster the "social tourism" that promotes the participation of the weaker classes and can thus be an effective instrument to combat poverty and frailty, providing jobs, safeguarding resources, and promoting equality. This form of tourism is a cause of hope in a world in which there is a noticeable gap between those who have everything and those who suffer hunger, famine, and drought. I hope that the reflection occasioned by this World Day of Tourism, thanks to the theme suggested, will succeed in influencing the lifestyle of numerous tourists in a positive way, so that each one may make his or her own contribution to the well-being of all, which is ultimately the well-being of each one.

Lastly, I address an invitation to young people so that through

16. John Paul II, *Centesimus Annus,* n. 37.

17. Benedict XVI, Address during the Welcoming Ceremony and Meeting with Authorities of State, Apostolic Journey to France, Paris, September 12, 2008.

your institutions you may become supporters and champions of lifestyles that aim at an appreciation of nature and its defense, in a correct ecological perspective, as I stressed several times on the occasion of the World Youth Day in Sydney last July. It is also the task of new generations to promote healthy and supportive tourism that bans consumerism and the waste of the earth's resources, to make room for gestures of solidarity and friendship, of knowledge and understanding. In this way tourism can become a privileged educational instrument in peaceful coexistence. May God help you in your work. For my part, rest assured of my remembrance in prayer, as with affection I impart the apostolic blessing to those of you present here, to your loved ones, and to the members of your praiseworthy institutions.

## The Use of Alternative Energies Contributes to Mankind's Desire to Be Better Stewards of God's Creation

From Address to Her Excellency Mrs. Elín Flygenring,
New Ambassador of the Republic of Iceland to the Holy See,
December 18, 2008

On the global scene, the Holy See appreciates the interest your country has shown in favoring a greater involvement of the international community in the promotion of peace through the defense of human rights and the rule of law, in the struggle against poverty and especially in the protection of the environment. Your country's experience and technological expertise in the use of alternative energies can be of great service to other populations and contribute to mankind's desire to be better stewards of God's creation. I likewise cannot fail to commend Iceland's concern for those who suffer the effects of war and underdevelopment which has made your population generously open in receiving refugees and, among other initiatives, eager to see international trade established on a more equitable basis.

## Man Knows the Advantage That the Universe Has over Him; the Universe, Instead, Knows Nothing

From Address to the Members of the Pontifical
Academy for Life on the Occasion of the Fifteenth
General Assembly, February 21, 2009

Ever since the mid-nineteenth century when the Augustinian Abbot, Gregor Mendel, discovered the laws of the heredity of characteristics, for which he is considered the founder of genetics, this science has truly taken giant steps in the understanding of that language which is at the foundation of biological information and determines the development of a living being. It is for this reason that modern genetics has a particularly important place in the biological disciplines that have contributed to the wonderful development of the knowledge of the invisible architecture of the human body and the cellular and molecular processes that dictate its multiple activities. Science today has succeeded in revealing both the different hidden mechanisms of human physiology and the processes linked to the appearance of certain defects inherited from the parents. It has also revealed processes that make some people more exposed to the risk of contracting a disease. This knowledge, the result of intelligence and the efforts of countless experts, has made possible not only a more effective and early diagnosis of genetic diseases but also treatment destined to relieve the sufferings of the sick and, in some cases even to restore the hope of recovering their health. Since the sequencing of the entire human genome became available, the difference between one person and another and between the different human populations has also become the object of genetic research. This has permitted us to glimpse the possibility of new achievements.

The context of research still remains very open today and every day new horizons, still largely unexplored, are disclosed. The efforts of the researcher in these most enigmatic and precious areas demand special support; for this reason, collaboration among the different sciences is a support that can never be lacking in order to achieve results that are effective and at the same time achieve authentic progress for all humanity. This complementarity allows one to avoid the risk of a widespread genetic reductionism which tends to identify the person exclusively in terms of genetic information and interactions with the environment. It must be stressed that man will always be greater than all the elements that form his body; indeed, he carries within him the power of thought which always aspires to the truth about himself and about the world. The words of Blaise Pascal, a great thinker who was also a gifted scientist charged with significance, spring to mind: "Man is only a reed, the most feeble thing in nature, but he is a thinking reed. The entire universe need not arm itself to crush him. A vapor, a drop of water suffices to kill him. But, if the universe were to crush him, man would still be more noble than that which killed him, because he knows that he dies and he knows the advantage that the universe has over him; the universe, instead, knows nothing."[18]

Every human being, therefore, is far more than a unique combination of genetic information that is transmitted by his or her parents. Human generation can never be reduced to the mere reproduction of a new individual of the human species, as happens with any animal.

The arrival of each person in the world is always a new creation. The words of a psalm recall this with profound wisdom: "For it was you who created my being; knit me together in my mother's womb . . . my body held no secret from you when I was being fashioned in secret" (Ps 139 [138]:13, 15). Consequently, if one wishes to enter into the mystery of human life, no branch of science must isolate itself, claiming to have the last word. Rather, it must participate in the common vocation to reach the truth, though with the different methodologies and subject matter proper to each science. Your congress, however, analyzed not only the great challenges that genetics must tackle but also extended its constitution to the risks of eugenics, certainly not a new practice and which in the past has been employed in unprecedented forms of authentic discrimination and violence. The disapproval of eugenics used with violence by a state regime or as the result of hatred for a race or a people is so deeply rooted in consciences that it was formally expressed in the Universal Declaration of Human Rights. Despite this, still today disturbing manifestations of this odious practice that presents itself with various features are appearing. Of course, the

18. Blaise Pascal, *Pensées* (1670), n. 347.

eugenic and racial ideologies that humiliated man in the past and caused tremendous suffering are not being proposed again, but a new mentality is being introduced that tends to justify a different view of life and personal dignity founded on personal desires and individual rights. Hence there is a tendency to give priority to functional ability, efficiency, perfection, and physical beauty to the detriment of life's other dimensions which are deemed unworthy. The respect that is due to every human being, even bearing a developmental defect or a genetic disease that might manifest itself during life, is thus weakened while children whose life is considered not worth living are penalized from the moment of conception.

It is necessary to reiterate that every form of discrimination practiced by any authority with regard to persons, peoples, or races on the basis of differences traceable to real or presumed genetic factors is an attack on the whole of humanity. What must be strongly reaffirmed is the equal dignity of every human being by the very fact that he has been born. A person's biological, mental, and cultural development or state of health must never become a discriminatory factor. On the contrary, it is necessary to consolidate the culture of acceptance and love showing real solidarity toward those who suffer. It must break down the barriers that society often builds by discriminating against those who are disabled or affected by pathologies, or, worse, even reaching the selection and rejection of life in the name of an abstract ideal of health and physical perfection. If the human being is reduced to an object of experimental manipulation from the very earliest stages of his development this means that biotechnological medicine has surrendered to the will of the stronger. Trust in science must not make one forget the primacy of ethics when human life is at stake.

I am confident, dear friends, that your research in this sector may continue with the due scientific commitment and attention that the ethical factor demands on such important and crucial matters for the coherent development of personal existence. This is the hope with which I desire to conclude this meeting. As I invoke upon your work an abundance of heavenly light, I impart with affection a special apostolic blessing to you all.

## Even the Decisions of Individuals, Families, and Local Administrations Are Fundamental for the Preservation of the Environment

From Angelus, January 1, 2010

Today the Lord grants us to begin a new year in his Name and under the gaze of Mary Most Holy, the solemnity of whose Divine Motherhood we are celebrating today. I am glad to meet you for this first Angelus of 2010. I address those of you who have gathered in large numbers in St. Peter's Square and also those who have joined us in our prayer via radio and television. I wish for you all that the year which has just begun may be a time in which, with the Lord's help, we may satisfy Christ and God's will, and thus also improve this world of ours.

One objective that may be shared by everyone, an indispensable condition for peace, is the administration of the earth's natural resources fairly and wisely. "If You Want to Cultivate Peace, Protect Creation" is the timely theme to which I have dedicated my message for today's forty-third World Day of Peace. When the message was published, the heads of state and government were meeting in Copenhagen for the summit on the climate at which, once again, the urgent need for concerted approaches at the global level became apparent. At this moment, however, I would like to stress the importance that the decisions of individuals, families, and local administrations also have in the preservation of the environment. "We can no longer do without a real change of outlook which will result in new lifestyles."[19] In fact we are all responsible for the protection and care of creation. Therefore in this field too education is fundamental; to learn to respect nature; to be increasingly disposed to begin building peace "with far-reaching decisions on the part of individuals, families, communities, and states."[20]

If we must care for the creatures that surround us, what consideration we should have for people, our brothers and sisters! What respect for human life! On the first day of the year I would like to address an appeal to the consciences of all who belong to armed groups of any kind. I say to each and every one: stop, think, and abandon the path of violence! At the moment this step might seem impossible to you; but if you have the courage to take it, God will assist you and you will feel returning to your hearts the joy of peace which perhaps you have forgotten for some time. I entrust this appeal to the intercession of Mary, the Most Holy Mother of God. The liturgy today reminds us that eight days after the birth of the Child, together with Joseph, her husband, she had him circumcised, in accordance with Mo-

19. Benedict XVI, Message for the 2010 World Day of Peace, n. 11, January 1, 2010.
20. Ibid.

saic law, and called him Jesus, the name given to him by the Angel (cf. Lk 2:21). This name, which means "God saves," is the fulfillment of God's revelation. Jesus is the Face of God, he is the blessing for every person and for all peoples, he is peace for the world. Thank you, Blessed Mother, who gave birth to the Savior, the Prince of Peace!

## *Social Responsibility Means More Attention to the Needs of Workers, the Good of the Community, and the Respect of the Environment*

From Address to the Directors and Personnel of the Municipal
Electricity and Water Board (ACEA), February 6, 2010

I would also like to express my pleasure at your project of cooperation with the John Paul II Foundation for the Sahel, in the endeavor to respond to the emergency in water and energy resources in their developing countries.

I have also seen with great interest your "Charter of Values" and "Ethical Code" that recall the principles of responsibility, transparency, correctness, and the spirit of service and collaboration that ACEA invokes. These are the guidelines that this board desires to recall and on which it wishes to build its image and reputation.

You have just concluded the celebrations for the centenary of ACEA. Indeed, one hundred years have passed since that 10 September 1909, when with a popular referendum the citizens of Rome decided that public lighting and collective transportation should be municipalized. Since that day your board has developed together with Rome. It has been a long and fascinating journey, full of both challenges and triumphs. It is enough to remember how complicated it was to guarantee essential services to ever wider social sectors, to new neighborhoods that have often developed in a chaotic and illegal manner in a city that was changing and expanding out of all proportion. Thus, in the course of the years, we can say that the relationship between the city and ACEA has become ever closer, thanks, especially, to the many services that the company has supplied and continues to supply to the city, sustaining and encouraging its transformation into a modern metropolis.

This centenary celebration has ended in a period full of difficulties, marked by a serious international crisis that has led the world to rethink a model of development based primarily on finance and profit, in order to refocus human activity on our capacity to produce, to innovate, to think, and to build the future. As I emphasized in the encyclical *Caritas in Veritate,* it is important to increase awareness in the business world of the need for a broader "social responsibility" that will impel it to continue to give proper consideration to the expectations and needs of their workers, customers, suppliers, and the entire community and to pay special attention to the environment.[21] Thus the production of goods and services will not be exclusively bound to the search for financial gain but also to the promotion of the common good. I rejoice that the history of the past hundred years has not only been expressed in the numerical terms of ever

21. Benedict XVI, *Caritas in Veritate,* n. 40.

greater competitiveness but also in a moral commitment that strives to pursue the well-being of all.

In the spirit of service that characterizes ACEA I would like to express my appreciation of all that ACEA has achieved, thanks to the professional skill of its employees, in illuminating the monuments that make Rome unique in the world. In this regard, I would like to recall with gratitude the material assistance provided on the occasion of the celebrations for the eightieth anniversary of the foundation of Vatican City State. Numerous churches, starting with St. Peter's Basilica, have also been enhanced by skillful lighting which brings out what human beings have been able to achieve in order to express their faith in Christ, "the true light that enlightens every man" (Jn 1:9).

I also appreciate ACEA's commitment to protecting the environment by means of the sustainable management of natural resources, reduction of the environmental impact [of its activities], and respect for creation. However, it is equally important to promote a human ecology which can make both the workplace and personal relations worthy of the human being. In this regard I would like to reaffirm what I said in the Message for the World Day of Peace this year on "the adoption of a model of development based on the centrality of the human person, on the promotion and sharing of the common good, on responsibility, on a realization of our need for a changed lifestyle."[22]

In Rome, as in every large city, one feels the effects of a culture that exacerbates the concept of the individual: often people live closed into themselves, wrapped up in their own problems,

22. Benedict XVI, Message for the World Day of Peace 2010, n. 9, January 1, 2010.

distracted by the many worries that crowd the mind and prevent men and women from perceiving the simple joys present in each person's life. The preservation of creation, a task that the Creator entrusted to humankind (cf. Gn 2:15), also implies the safeguarding of those sentiments of goodness, generosity, correctness, and honesty which God has placed in the heart of every human being who is created in his "image and likeness" (cf. Gn 1:26).

Lastly, I wish to address to those present an invitation to look to Christ, the perfect man and always to take his actions as an example in order to grow in humanity and thus to develop a city with an ever more human face, in which everyone is seen as a person, a spiritual being in relation with others. Thanks too to your commitment to improving interpersonal relationships and the quality of work, Rome may continue its role as a beacon of civilization which has distinguished it down the centuries.

## Science as a Place of Dialogue, the Meeting between Man and Nature and Potentially Even between Man and His Creator

From Address to Participants in the Plenary Session of the Pontifical Academy of Sciences, October 28, 2010

The history of science in the twentieth century is one of undoubted achievement and major advances. Unfortunately, the popular image of twentieth-century science is sometimes characterized otherwise, in two extreme ways. On the one hand, science is posited by some as a panacea, proven by its notable achievements in the last century. Its innumerable advances were in fact so encompassing and so rapid that they seemed to confirm the point of view that science might answer all the questions of man's existence, and even of his highest aspirations. On the other hand, there are those who fear science and who distance themselves from it, because of sobering developments such as the construction and terrifying use of nuclear weapons.

Science, of course, is not defined by either of these extremes. Its task was and remains a patient yet passionate search for the truth about the cosmos, about nature, and about the constitution of the human being. In this search, there have been many successes and failures, triumphs and setbacks. The developments of science have been both uplifting, as when the complexity of nature and its phenomena were discovered, exceeding our expectations, and humbling, as when some of the theories we thought might have explained those phenomena once and for all proved only partial. Nonetheless, even provisional results constitute a real contribution to unveiling the correspondence between the intellect and natural realities, on which later generations may build further.

The progress made in scientific knowledge in the twentieth century, in all its various disciplines, has led to a greatly improved awareness of the place that man and this planet occupy in the universe. In all sciences, the common denominator continues to be the notion of experimentation as an organized method for observing nature. In the last century, man certainly made more progress—if not always in his knowledge of himself and of God, then certainly in his knowledge of the macro- and microcosms—than in the entire previous history of humanity.

Our meeting here today, dear friends, is a proof of the Church's esteem for ongoing scientific research and of her gratitude for scientific endeavor, which she both encourages and benefits from. In our own day, scientists themselves appreciate more and more the need to be open to philosophy if they are to discover the logical and epistemological foundation for their methodology and their conclusions. For her part, the Church is convinced that scientific activity ultimately benefits from the recognition of man's spiritual dimension and his quest for ultimate answers that allow for the acknowledgment of a world existing independently from us, which we do not fully understand and which we can only comprehend in so far as we grasp its inherent logic. Scientists do not create the world; they learn about it and attempt to imitate it, following the laws and intelligibility that nature manifests to us. The scientist's experience as a human being is therefore that of perceiving a constant, a law, a *logos* that he has not created but that he has instead observed: in fact, it leads us to admit the existence of an all-powerful Reason, which is other than that of man, and which sustains the world. This is the meeting point between the natural sciences and religion. As a result, science becomes a place of dialogue, a meeting between man and nature and, potentially, even between man and his Creator.

As we look to the twenty-first century, I would like to propose two thoughts for further reflection. First, as increasing accomplishments of the sciences deepen our wonder of the complexity of nature, the need for an interdisciplinary approach tied with philosophical reflection leading to a synthesis is more and more perceived. Secondly, scientific achievement in this new century should always be informed by the imperatives of fraternity and peace, helping to solve the great problems of humanity, and directing everyone's efforts toward the true good of man and the integral development of the peoples of the world. The positive outcome of twenty-first-century science will surely depend in large measure on the scientist's ability to search for truth and apply discoveries in a way that goes hand in hand with the search for what is just and good.

With these sentiments, I invite you to direct your gaze toward Christ, the uncreated Wisdom, and to recognize in His face the *Logos* of the Creator of all things. Renewing my good wishes for your work, I willingly impart my apostolic blessing.

## Unlimited Speculation Has a Negative Impact on the Environment and on Man Himself

From Address to Participants in the Meeting
Promoted by the Pontifical Council for Justice and
Peace on the Fiftieth Anniversary of the Encyclical
*Mater et Magistra*, May 16, 2011

However, no less worrying are the phenomena linked to a financial system which, after the most acute phase of the crisis, has returned to the frenzied practice of drawing up credit contracts that often allow unlimited speculation. The phenomenon of harmful speculation occurs also in regard to staple foodstuffs, water, and land, ultimately further impoverishing those already living in borderline situations.

Likewise, it is seen in the increase in the prices of basic energy resources, with the consequent search for alternative forms of energy prompted, on occasion, by exclusively short-term financial interests, which can result in a negative impact on the environment, as well as on man himself.

## Ecology of Man, Ecology of the Environment

From Address to the Bundestag,
Apostolic Journey to Germany,
September 22, 2011

But the invitation to give this address was extended to me as pope, as the bishop of Rome, who bears the highest responsibility for Catholic Christianity. In issuing this invitation you are acknowledging the role that the Holy See plays as a partner within the community of peoples and states. Setting out from this international responsibility that I hold, I should like to propose to you some thoughts on the foundations of a free state of law.

Allow me to begin my reflections on the foundations of law [Recht] with a brief story from sacred scripture. In the First Book of Kings, it is recounted that God invited the young King Solomon, on his accession to the throne, to make a request. What will the young ruler ask for at this important moment? Success—wealth—long life  destruction of his enemies? He chooses none of these things. Instead, he asks for a listening heart so that he may govern God's people, and discern between good and evil (cf. 1 Kgs 3:9). Through this story, the Bible wants to tell us what should ultimately matter for a politician. His fundamental criterion and the motivation for his work as a politician must not be success, and certainly not material gain. Politics must be a striving for justice, and hence it has to establish the fundamental preconditions for peace. Naturally a politician will seek success, without which he would have no opportunity for effective political action at all. Yet success is subordinated to the criterion of justice, to the will to do what is right, and to the understanding of what is right. Success can also be seductive and thus can open up the path toward the falsification of what is right, toward the destruction of justice. "Without justice—what else is the state but a great band of robbers?" as St. Augustine once said. We Germans know from our own experience that these words are no empty specter. We have seen how power became divorced from right, how power opposed right and crushed it, so that the state became an instrument for destroying right—a highly organized band of robbers, capable of threatening the whole world and driving it to the edge of the abyss. To serve right and to fight against the dominion of wrong is and remains the fundamental task of the politician. At a moment in history when man has acquired previously inconceivable power, this task takes on a particular urgency. Man can destroy the world. He can manipulate himself. He can, so to speak, make human beings and he can deny them their humanity. How do we recognize what is right? How can we discern between good and evil, between what is truly right and what may appear right? Even now, Solomon's request remains the decisive issue facing politicians and politics today.

For most of the matters that need to be regulated by law, the support of the majority can serve as a sufficient criterion. Yet it is evident that for the fundamental issues of law, in which the dignity of man and of humanity is at stake, the majority principle is not enough: everyone in a position of responsibility must personally seek out the criteria to be followed when framing laws. In the third century, the great theologian Origen provided the following explanation for the resistance of Christians to certain legal systems: "Suppose that a man were living among the Scythians, whose laws are contrary to the divine law, and was compelled to live among them ... such a man for the sake of the true law, though illegal among the Scythians, would rightly form associations with like-minded people contrary to the laws of the Scythians."[23]

This conviction was what motivated resistance movements to act against the Nazi regime and other totalitarian regimes, thereby doing a great service to justice and to humanity as a whole. For these people, it was indisputably evident that the law in force was actually unlawful. Yet when it comes to the decisions of a democratic politician, the question of what now corresponds to the law of truth, what is actually right and may be enacted as law, is less obvious. In terms of the underlying anthropological issues, what is right and may be given the force of law is in no way simply self-evident today. The question of how to recognize what is truly right and thus to serve justice when framing laws has never been simple, and today in view of the vast extent of our knowledge and our capacity, it has become still harder.

How do we recognize what is right? In history, systems of law have almost always been based on religion: decisions re-

23. Origen of Alexandria, *Contra Celsum*, bk. 1, chap. 1; cf. Alfons Furst, "Monotheismus und Monarchie. Zum Zusammenhang von und Herrschaft in der Antike," *Theologie und Philosophie* 81 (2006): 321–38, quoted on 336; cf. also Joseph Ratzinger, *Die Einheit der Nationen: Eine Vision der Kirchenväter* (Salzburg and Munich: Pustet, 1971), 60.

garding what was to be lawful among men were taken with reference to the divinity. Unlike other great religions, Christianity has never proposed a revealed law to the state and to society, that is to say a juridical order derived from revelation. Instead, it has pointed to nature and reason as the true sources of law—and to the harmony of objective and subjective reason, which naturally presupposes that both spheres are rooted in the creative reason of God. Christian theologians thereby aligned themselves with a philosophical and juridical movement that began to take shape in the second century B.C. In the first half of that century, the social natural law developed by the Stoic philosophers came into contact with leading teachers of Roman law.[24] Through this encounter, the juridical culture of the West was born, which was and is of key significance for the juridical culture of mankind. This pre-Christian marriage between law and philosophy opened up the path that led via the Christian Middle Ages and the juridical developments of the Age of Enlightenment all the way to the Declaration of Human Rights and to our German Basic Law of 1949, with which our nation committed itself to "inviolable and inalienable human rights as the foundation of every human community, and of peace and justice in the world."

For the development of law and for the development of humanity, it was highly significant that Christian theologians aligned themselves against the religious law associated with polytheism and on the side of philosophy, and that they acknowledged reason and nature in their interrelation as the uni-

---

24. Cf. Wolfgang Waldstein, *Ins Herz geschrieben: Das Naturrecht als Fundament einer menschlichen Gesellschaft* (Augsburg: Sankt Ulrich Verlag, 2010), 11ff., 31–61.

versally valid source of law. This step had already been taken by St. Paul in the Letter to the Romans, when he said: "When Gentiles who have not the Law [the Torah of Israel] do by nature what the law requires, they are a law to themselves … they show that what the law requires is written on their hearts, while their conscience also bears witness" (Rom 2:14f.). Here we see the two fundamental concepts of nature and conscience, where conscience is nothing other than Solomon's listening heart, reason that is open to the language of being. If this seemed to offer a clear explanation of the foundations of legislation up to the time of the Enlightenment, up to the time of the Declaration on Human Rights after the Second World War and the framing of our Basic Law, there has been a dramatic shift in the situation in the last half-century. The idea of natural law is today viewed as a specifically Catholic doctrine, not worth bringing into the discussion in a non-Catholic environment, so that one feels almost ashamed even to mention the term. Let me outline briefly how this situation arose. Fundamentally it is because of the idea that an unbridgeable gulf exists between "is" and "ought." An "ought" can never follow from an "is," because the two are situated on completely different planes. The reason for this is that in the meantime, the positivist understanding of nature has come to be almost universally accepted. If nature—in the words of Hans Kelsen—is viewed as "an aggregate of objective data linked together in terms of cause and effect," then indeed no ethical indication of any kind can be derived from it.[25] A positivist conception of nature as purely functional, as the natural

25. Cf. ibid., 15–21.

sciences consider it to be, is incapable of producing any bridge to ethics and law, but once again yields only functional answers. The same also applies to reason, according to the positivist understanding that is widely held to be the only genuinely scientific one. Anything that is not verifiable or falsifiable, according to this understanding, does not belong to the realm of reason strictly understood. Hence ethics and religion must be assigned to the subjective field, and they remain extraneous to the realm of reason in the strict sense of the word. Where positivist reason dominates the field to the exclusion of all else—and that is broadly the case in our public mindset—then the classical sources of knowledge for ethics and law are excluded. This is a dramatic situation which affects everyone, and on which a public debate is necessary. Indeed, an essential goal of this address is to issue an urgent invitation to launch one.

The positivist approach to nature and reason, the positivist world view in general, is a most important dimension of human knowledge and capacity that we may in no way dispense with. But in and of itself it is not a sufficient culture corresponding to the full breadth of the human condition. Where positivist reason considers itself the only sufficient culture and banishes all other cultural realities to the status of subcultures, it diminishes man, indeed it threatens his humanity. I say this with Europe specifically in mind, where there are concerted efforts to recognize only positivism as a common culture and a common basis for law-making, reducing all the other insights and values of our culture to the level of subculture, with the result that Europe vis-à-vis other world cultures is left in a state of culturelessness and at the same time extremist and radical movements emerge to fill the vacuum. In its self-proclaimed exclusivity, the positivist reason which recognizes nothing beyond mere functionality resembles a concrete bunker with no windows, in which we ourselves provide lighting and atmospheric conditions, being no longer willing to obtain either from God's wide world. And yet we cannot hide from ourselves the fact that even in this artificial world, we are still covertly drawing upon God's raw materials, which we refashion into our own products. The windows must be flung open again, we must see the wide world, the sky, and the earth once more and learn to make proper use of all this.

But how are we to do this? How do we find our way out into the wide world, into the big picture? How can reason rediscover its true greatness, without being sidetracked into irrationality? How can nature reassert itself in its true depth, with all its demands, with all its directives? I would like to recall one of the developments in recent political history, hoping that I will neither be misunderstood, nor provoke too many one-sided polemics. I would say that the emergence of the ecological movement in German politics since the 1970s, while it has not exactly flung open the windows, nevertheless was and continues to be a cry for fresh air which must not be ignored or pushed aside, just because too much of it is seen to be irrational. Young people had come to realize that something is wrong in our relationship with nature, that matter is not just raw material for us to shape at will, but that the earth has a dignity of its own and that we must follow its directives. In saying this, I am clearly not promoting any particular political party—nothing could be further from my mind. If something is wrong in our relationship with reality, then we must all reflect seriously on the whole situation and we are all prompted to question the very foundations of our culture. Allow me to dwell a little longer on this point. The importance of ecology is no longer disputed. We must listen to the language of nature and we must answer accordingly. Yet I would like to underline a point that seems to me to be neglected, today as in the past: there is also an ecology of man. Man too has a nature that he must respect and that he cannot manipulate at will. Man is not merely self-creating freedom. Man does not create himself. He is intellect and will, but he is also nature, and his will is rightly ordered if he respects his nature, listens to it, and accepts himself for who he is, as one who did not create himself. In this way, and in no other, is true human freedom fulfilled.

Let us come back to the fundamental concepts of nature and reason, from which we set out. The great proponent of legal positivism, Kelsen, at the age of eighty-four—in 1965—abandoned the dualism of "is" and "ought." (I find it comforting that rational thought is evidently still possible at the age of eighty-four!) Previously he had said that norms can only come from the will. Nature therefore could only contain norms, he adds, if a will had put them there. But this, he says, would presuppose a Creator God, whose will had entered into nature. "Any attempt to discuss the truth of this belief is utterly futile," he observed.[26] Is it really? I find myself asking. Is it really pointless to wonder whether the objective reason that manifests itself in nature does not presuppose a creative reason, a *Creator Spiritus*?

At this point Europe's cultural heritage ought to come to our

26. Ibid., 19.

assistance. The conviction that there is a Creator God is what gave rise to the idea of human rights, the idea of the equality of all people before the law, the recognition of the inviolability of human dignity in every single person, and the awareness of people's responsibility for their actions. Our cultural memory is shaped by these rational insights. To ignore it or dismiss it as a thing of the past would be to dismember our culture totally and to rob it of its completeness. The culture of Europe arose from the encounter between Jerusalem, Athens, and Rome—from the encounter between Israel's monotheism, the philosophical reason of the Greeks, and Roman law. This three-way encounter has shaped the inner identity of Europe. In the awareness of man's responsibility before God and in the acknowledgment of the inviolable dignity of every single human person, it has established criteria of law: it is these criteria that we are called to defend at this moment in our history.

As he assumed the mantle of office, the young King Solomon was invited to make a request. How would it be if we, the law-makers of today, were invited to make a request? What would we ask for? I think that, even today, there is ultimately nothing else we could wish for but a listening heart—the capacity to discern between good and evil, and thus to establish true law, to serve justice and peace. I thank you for your attention!

*The Church Must Encourage Governments
to Protect the Fundamental Goods Which
Are the Earth and Water*

From Post-Synodal Apostolic Exhortation *Africae Munus*
on the Church in Africa in Service to Reconciliation,
Justice, and Peace, November 19, 2011

## B. RESPECT FOR CREATION
## AND THE ECOSYSTEM

79. Together with the synod fathers, I ask all the members of the Church to work and speak out in favor of an economy that cares for the poor and is resolutely opposed to an unjust order which, under the pretext of reducing poverty, has often helped to aggravate it.[27] God has given Africa important natural resources. Given the chronic poverty of its people, who suffer the effects of exploitation and embezzlement of funds both locally and abroad, the opulence of certain groups shocks the human conscience. Organized for the creation of wealth in their homelands, and not infrequently with the complicity of those in power in Africa, these groups too often ensure their own prosperity at the expense of the well-being of the local population.[28] Acting in concert with all other components of civil society, the Church must speak out against the unjust order that prevents

27. Second Special Assembly for Africa of the Synod of Bishops, Final List of Propositions (October 23, 2009), Propositions 17 and 29.
28. Cf. Second Special Assembly for Africa of the Synod of Bishops, Final Message (October 23, 2009).

the peoples of Africa from consolidating their economies[29] and "from developing according to their cultural characteristics."[30] Moreover, it is incumbent upon the Church to strive that "every people may be the principal agent of its own economic and social progress... and may help to bring about the universal common good as an active and responsible member of the human family, on an equal footing with other peoples."[31]

80. Some business men and women, governments, and financial groups are involved in programs of exploitation which pollute the environment and cause unprecedented desertification. Serious damage is done to nature, to the forests, to flora and fauna, and countless species risk extinction. All of this threatens the entire ecosystem and consequently the survival of humanity.[32] I call upon the Church in Africa to encourage political leaders to protect such fundamental goods as land and water for the human life of present and future generations[33] and for peace between peoples.

29. Cf. Benedict XVI, *Caritas in Veritate,* n. 42; cf. Second Special Assembly for Africa of the Synod of Bishops, Final List of Propositions, Proposition 15.

30. Second Ordinary General Assembly of the Synod of Bishops, Document *Justice in the World* (November 30, 1971), Proposition 8a.

31. Ibid., Propositions 8b and 8c.

32. Cf. Second Special Assembly for Africa of the Synod of Bishops, Final List of Propositions, Proposition 22.

33. Cf. ibid., Proposition 30.

PART 3

---

# HUNGER, POVERTY, AND THE EARTH'S RESOURCES

## Nourishing the World's Population with Respect for Biodiversity

From Message of His Holiness Benedict XVI to
Mr. Jacques Diouf, Director General of the Food and
Agriculture Organization (FAO), on the Occasion of
World Food Day 2005, October 12, 2005

This year, which marks the sixtieth anniversary of the establishment of the Food and Agriculture Organization of the United Nations, the celebration of World Food Day reminds us that hunger and malnutrition unfortunately feature among the worst scandals that still affect the life of the human family. This makes the FAO's action, under your direction, ever more urgent.

The millions of people whose very lives are at risk because they lack the minimum basic food call for the attention of the international community, because it is the common duty of us all to care for our brothers and sisters.

Indeed, famine is not entirely due to geographical and climatic situations or to the unfavorable circumstances linked to harvests. It is also caused by human beings themselves and by their selfishness, which is expressed by gaps in social organization, by rigidity in economic structures all too often oriented solely to profit, and even by practices against human life and ideological systems that reduce the person, deprived of his fundamental dignity, to being a mere instrument.

True world development, organized and integral, which everyone hopes for, requires on the contrary an objective knowledge of human situations, the identification of the real causes of poverty, and practical responses whose priority is the appropriate formation of each person and community. Thus, the authentic freedom and responsibility that are proper to human action will be put into practice.

The theme chosen for this day, "Agriculture and the Dialogue of Cultures," is an invitation to consider dialogue as an effective instrument to create the conditions for food security. Dialogue requires people and nations to join forces to serve the common good. The convergence of all the protagonists, combined with effective cooperation, can help to build *true peace,* making it possible to overcome the recurrent temptations of war that stem from differences in cultural outlook, race, or level of development.

It is also important to be directly alert to human situations, with the aim of maintaining the diversity of development models and forms of technical assistance in accordance with the particular conditions of each country and each community, whether it is a matter of economic or environmental or even social, cultural, and spiritual conditions.

Technical progress will only be truly effective if it has a place in a broader perspective that centers on man and is concerned to consider all his needs and aspirations, for, as scripture says: "Not on bread alone is man to live" (cf. Dt 8:3; Mt 4:4). This will also enable every people to draw from its patrimony of values in order to share its material and spiritual riches for the benefit of all.

The ambitious and complex goals that your organization

sets itself will not be achieved unless the protection of human dignity, the first and last of the fundamental rights, becomes the criterion that inspires and directs all its efforts.

The Catholic Church, which also participates in actions that aim at truly harmonious development, in collaboration with the partners present on the spot, hopes to encourage the FAO's activity and efforts in order to initiate a true dialogue of cultures at her level and thereby to contribute to increasing the ability to nourish the world population, with respect for biodiversity. In fact, the human being must not rashly compromise the natural balance, a result of the order of creation, but on the contrary must take care to pass on to future generations an earth able to feed them.

In this spirit, I ask the Almighty to bless the mission of the FAO, which is so necessary, and the commitment of its directors and officials, with a view to guaranteeing to each member of the human family his or her daily bread.

### Without Solidarity between Countries There Is a Risk of Impeding the Work of International Organizations Committed to Fighting Hunger and Malnutrition

From Message to the Director General of the FAO for the
Celebration of World Food Day 2006, October 16, 2006

The annual celebration of World Food Day, sponsored by the Food and Agriculture Organization of the United Nations, is an opportunity to review the numerous activities of this organization, specifically with regard to its twofold aim: to provide adequate nutrition for our brothers and sisters throughout the world and to consider the obstacles to this work caused by difficult situations and attitudes contrary to solidarity.

This year's chosen theme—"Investing in Agriculture for Food Security"—focuses our attention on the agricultural sector and invites us to reflect on the various factors that hinder the fight against hunger, many of them man-made. Not enough attention is given to the needs of agriculture, and this both upsets the natural order of creation and compromises respect for human dignity.

In Christian tradition, agricultural labor takes on a deeper meaning, both because of the effort and hardship that it involves and also because it offers a privileged experience of God's presence and his love for his creatures. Christ himself uses agricultural images to speak of the Kingdom, thereby showing a great respect for this form of labor.

Today, we think especially of those who have had to abandon their farmlands because of conflicts, natural disasters, and because of society's neglect of the agricultural sector. The "promotion of justice through efforts to bring about openness of mind and will to the demands of the common good is something which concerns the Church deeply."[1]

It is now ten years since my venerable predecessor, Pope John Paul II, inaugurated the World Food Summit. This gives us an opportunity to look back and take stock of the inadequate attention given to the agricultural sector and the effects this has on

---

1. Benedict XVI, Encyclical Letter *Deus Caritas Est* (December 25, 2005), n. 28.

rural communities. Solidarity is the key to identifying and eliminating the causes of poverty and underdevelopment.

Very often, international action to combat hunger ignores the *human factor,* and priority is given instead to technical and socio-economic aspects. Local communities need to be involved in choices and decisions concerning land use, since farmland is being diverted increasingly to other purposes, often with damaging effects on the environment and the long-term viability of the land. If the human person is treated as the protagonist, it becomes clear that short-term economic gains must be placed within the context of better long-term planning for food security, with regard to both quantity and quality.

The order of creation demands that priority be given to those human activities that do not cause irreversible damage to nature, but which instead are woven into the social, cultural, and religious fabric of the different communities. In this way, a sober balance is achieved between consumption and the sustainability of resources.

The *rural family* needs to regain its rightful place at the heart of the social order. The moral principles and values which govern it belong to the heritage of humanity, and must take priority over legislation. They are concerned with individual conduct, relations between husband and wife and between generations, and the sense of family solidarity. Investment in the agricultural sector has to allow the family to assume its proper place and function, avoiding the damaging consequences of hedonism and materialism that can place marriage and family life at risk.

Education and formation programs in rural areas need to be broadly based, adequately resourced, and aimed at all age groups. Special attention should be given to the most vulnerable, especially women and the young. It is important to hand on to future generations not merely the technical aspects of production, nutrition, and protection of natural resources, but the values of the rural world.

In faithfully carrying out its mandate, the FAO makes a vital investment in agriculture, not only through adequate technical and specialized support, but also by broadening the dialogue that takes place among the national and international agencies involved in rural development. Individual initiatives should be incorporated within larger strategies aimed at combatting poverty and hunger. This can be of decisive importance if the nations and communities involved are to implement consistent programs and work toward a common goal.

Today more than ever, in the face of recurring crises and the pursuit of narrow self-interest, there has to be cooperation and solidarity between states, each of which should be attentive to the needs of its weakest citizens, who are the first to suffer from poverty. Without this solidarity, there is a risk of limiting or even impeding the work of international organizations that set out to fight hunger and malnutrition. In this way, they build up effectively the spirit of justice, harmony, and peace among peoples: *"opus iustitiae pax"* (cf. Is 32:17).

With these thoughts, Director General, I wish to invoke the Lord's blessing upon FAO, its member states, and upon all those who work so hard to support the agricultural sector and to promote rural development.

## A New Europe Free from the Unique Form of "Apostasy" from Itself

From Address to the Participants in the Convention Organized
by the Commission of the Bishops' Conferences of the
European Community (COMECE), March 24, 2007

Since March 1957, this continent has travelled a long road, which has led to the reconciliation of its two "lungs"—the East and the West—linked by a common history, but arbitrarily separated by a curtain of injustice. Economic integration has stimulated political unification and encouraged the continuing and strenuous search for an institutional structure adequate for a European Union that already numbers twenty-seven nations and aspires to become a global actor on the world scene.

During these years there has emerged an increasing awareness of the need to establish a healthy balance between the economic and social dimensions, through policies capable of producing wealth and increasing competitiveness, while not neglecting the legitimate expectations of the poor and the marginalized. Unfortunately, from a demographic point of view, one must note that Europe seems to be following a path that could lead to its departure from history. This not only places economic growth at risk; it could also create enormous difficulties for social cohesion and, above all, favor a dangerous form of individualism inattentive to future consequences. One could almost think that the European continent is in fact losing faith in its own future. As regards, for example, respect for the environment or the structured access to energy resources and investments, incentives for solidarity are slow in coming, not only in the international sphere but also in the national one. The process of European unification itself is evidently not shared by all, due to the prevailing impression that various "chapters" in the European project have been "written" without taking into account the aspirations of its citizens.

From all this it clearly emerges that an authentic European "common home" cannot be built without considering the identity of the people of this continent of ours. It is a question of a historical, cultural, and moral identity before being a geographic, economic, or political one; an identity comprised of a set of universal values that Christianity helped forge, thus giving Christianity not only a historical but a foundational role vis-à-vis Europe. These values, which make up the soul of the continent, must remain in the Europe of the third millennium as a "ferment" of civilization. If these values were to disappear, how could the "old" continent continue to function as a "leaven" for the entire world? If, for the fiftieth anniversary of the Treaty of Rome, the governments of the Union wish to "get nearer" to their citizens, how can they exclude an element essential to European identity such as Christianity, with which a vast majority of citizens continue to identify? Is it not surprising that today's Europe, while aspiring to be regarded as a community of values, seems ever more often to deny the very existence of universal and absolute values? Does not this unique form of "apostasy" from itself, even more than its apostasy from God, lead Europe to doubt its own identity? And so the opinion prevails that an "evaluation of the benefits" is the only way to moral discernment and that the common good is synonymous with compromise. In reality, if compromise can constitute a legitimate balance between different particular interests, it becomes a common evil whenever it involves agreements that dishonor human nature.

A community built without respect for the true dignity of the human being, disregarding the fact that every person is created in the image of God ends up doing no good to anyone. For this reason it seems ever more important that Europe be on guard against the pragmatic attitude, widespread today, which systematically justifies compromise on essential human values, as if it were the inevitable acceptance of a lesser evil. This kind of pragmatism, even when presented as balanced and realistic, is in reality neither, since it denies the dimension of values and ideals inherent in human nature. When non-religious and relativistic tendencies are woven into this pragmatism, Christians as such are eventually denied the very right to enter into the public discussion, or their contribution is discredited as an attempt to preserve unjustified privileges. In this historical hour and faced with the many challenges that confront it, the European Union, in order to be a valid guarantor of the rule of law and an efficient promoter of universal values, cannot but recognize clearly the certain existence of a stable and permanent human nature, source of common rights for all individuals, including those who deny them. In this context, the right to conscientious objection should be protected, every time fundamental human rights are violated.

Dear friends, I know how difficult it is for Christians to defend this truth of the human person. Nevertheless do not give in to fatigue or discouragement! You know that it is your duty, with God's help, to contribute to the consolidation of a new Europe which will be realistic but not cynical, rich in ideals and free from naïve illusions, inspired by the perennial and life-giving truth of the Gospel. Therefore, be actively present in the public debate on a European level, knowing that this discussion is now an integral part of the national debate. And to this commitment add effective cultural action. Do not bend to the logic of power as an end in itself! May Christ's admonition be a constant stimulus and support for you: "If the salt loses its flavor it is no longer good for anything, except to be thrown out and trampled by men" (cf. Mt 5:13). May the Lord make all your efforts fruitful and help you to recognize and use properly what is positive in today's civilization, while denouncing with courage all that is contrary to human dignity.

I am certain that God will bless the generous efforts of all who, in a spirit of service, work to build a common European home where every cultural, social, and political contribution is directed toward the common good. To you, already involved in different ways in this important human and evangelical undertaking, I express my support and my most fervent encouragement.

## When the Logic of Sharing and Solidarity Prevails It Is Possible to Direct the Course toward an Equitable and Sustainable Development

From Angelus, Castel Gandolfo, September 23, 2007

During the solemn Eucharistic celebration, by commenting on the liturgical texts, I was able to pause and reflect on the correct use of earthly goods, a theme the Evangelist Luke proposes for our attention this Sunday in various ways.

Telling the parable of the dishonest but very crafty administrator, Christ teaches his disciples the best way to use money and material riches, that is, to share them with the poor, thus acquiring their friendship, with a view to the Kingdom of Heaven. "Make friends for yourselves by means of unrighteous mammon," Jesus says, "so that when it fails they may receive you into the eternal habitations" (Lk 16:9).

Money is not "dishonest" in itself, but more than anything else it can close man in a blind egocentrism. It therefore concerns a type of work of "conversion" of economic goods: instead of using them only for self-interest, it is also necessary to think of the needs of the poor, imitating Christ himself, who, as St. Paul wrote: "Though he was rich, yet for your sake he became poor, so that by his poverty you might become rich" (2 Cor 8:9).

It seems paradoxical: Christ has not enriched us with his richness but with his poverty, with his love that brought him to give himself totally to us.

Here one could open up a vast and complex field of reflection on the theme of poverty and riches, also on a world scale, in which two logics of economics oppose each other: the logic of profit and that of the equal distribution of goods, which do not contradict each other if their relationship is well ordered.

Catholic social doctrine has always supported that equitable distribution of goods is a priority. Naturally, profit is legitimate and, in just measure, necessary for economic development.

In his encyclical *Centesimus Annus,* John Paul II wrote: "The modern business economy has positive aspects. Its basis is human freedom exercised in many other fields."[2] Yet, he adds that capitalism must not be considered as the only valid model of economic organization.[3] Starvation and ecological emergencies stand to denounce, with increasing evidence, that the logic of profit, if it prevails, increases the disproportion between rich and poor and leads to a ruinous exploitation of the planet.

Instead, when the logic of sharing and solidarity prevails, it is possible to correct the course and direct it toward an equitable, sustainable development.

## *The Right to Food*

From Message to Mr. Jacques Diouf, Director General of FAO,
on the Occasion of World Food Day 2007, October 4, 2007

1. This year the United Nations' Food and Agriculture Organization, which you direct, invites the international community, remembering once again its foundation, to tackle one of

2. John Paul II, *Centesimus Annus,* n. 32.
3. Ibid., n. 35.

the gravest challenges of our time: freeing millions of human beings from hunger, whose lives are in danger due to a lack of daily bread.

The theme chosen for this day, "The Right to Food," fittingly opens the reflections that the international community is preparing to make on the occasion of the sixtieth anniversary of the Universal Declaration of Human Rights. This coincidence helps us to recall the importance that the right to food has for the realization of other rights, beginning above all with the fundamental right to life.

We must observe that the endeavors made until now have not significantly diminished the numbers of those suffering from hunger in the world, even though all know that food is a primary right. This is perhaps due to the fact that one tends to be solely and principally motivated by technical and economic considerations, forgetting the primary, ethical dimension of "feeding the hungry."

This priority concerns the sentiments of compassion and solidarity proper to the human being, which includes sharing with others not only material goods, but also the love which all need. In effect, we give too little if we offer only material things.

2. The available data show that the non-fulfillment of the right to food is not only due to natural causes, but also and above all to situations provoked by the conduct of men and women that lead to a general deterioration of social, economic, and human standards.

Increasingly, there are always more people who, because of poverty and bloody conflicts, feel obligated to leave their own home and loved ones in order to search for support outside their own country. In spite of international pledges, many of these people are refused.

Among the mature members of the community of nations, however, a strong awareness is needed that considers food as a universal right of all human beings, without distinction or discrimination.

3. The objective of eradicating hunger and at the same time of being able to provide healthy and sufficient food also demands specific methods and actions that mean a wise use of resources that respect creation's patrimony.

The result of working in this direction will benefit not only science, research, and technology, but also take into account the cycles and rhythm of nature known to the inhabitants of rural areas, thus protecting the traditional customs of the indigenous communities, leaving aside egotistical and exclusively economic motivations.

The right to food, with all that this implies, has an immediate repercussion on both the individual and communal dimensions, which bring together entire peoples and human groups. I am thinking in a special way of the situation of children—the main victims of this tragedy—who at times have obstacles to their physical and psychological development and in many instances are forced to work or are enlisted in armed groups in exchange for a little food.

In such cases, I place my hope in the initiatives that have been proposed on many levels in favor of school food programs and which permit the entire community, whose survival is threatened by hunger, to look with great hope to the future.

A common and concrete commitment is therefore urgently

needed in which all members of society, both in the individual as well as the international spheres, feel duty-bound to work together in order to actualize the right to food, for failure to do so constitutes a clear violation of human dignity and of the rights which derive from it.

4. Knowledge of the problems of the agricultural world and of a lack of food, demonstrated by a capacity to propose plans and programs to find solutions, is a fundamental merit of the FAO and testifies to the acute sensibility for the aspirations of those conditions put forward for a more human life.

At this time when there are so many similar problems, it would also be well to find new initiatives that can contribute to alleviating the drama of hunger, and I encourage you to continue to work so that food may be guaranteed that responds to actual needs, and in such a way that every person, created in the image of God, may grow conformed to his true human dimension.

The Catholic Church feels close to you in this endeavor and, throughout your diverse institutions, desires to continue to collaborate in order to sustain the aspirations and hopes of those persons and those peoples for which the work of the FAO is directed. These are, Mr. Director General, some reflections that I wish to bring to the attention of those who, with different responsibilities, work to offer the human family a future free of the drama of hunger, and at the same time, I invoke upon you and your work the constant Blessing of the Most High.

## *Justly Administering the Fruits of Creation*

From Message to Participants Attending the
High-Level Conference on World Food Security:
The Challenges of Climate Change and Bioenergy,
Organized by the United Nations Food and
Agriculture Organization, June 2, 2008

Yet, how can one remain insensitive to the appeals of those who, on the various continents, are not able to feed themselves enough to live? Poverty and malnutrition are not a mere fatality caused by adverse environmental circumstances or by disastrous natural calamities. On the other hand, considerations of an exclusively technical or economic character must not prevail over the rights of justice toward those who suffer from hunger. "The right to nutrition responds principally to an ethical motivation: 'give the hungry to eat' (cf. Mt 25:35), that prompts a sharing of material goods as a sign of the love which we all need.... This primary right to nutrition is intrinsically linked to the safeguarding and to the defense of human life, the solid and inviolable rock upon which the whole edifice of human rights is founded."[4] Each person has the right to life: therefore it is necessary to promote the effective actualization of such rights and the populations that suffer from lack of food must be helped to gradually become capable of satisfying their own needs for sufficient and healthy nutrition.

At this particular moment, in which food security is threat-

---

4. Benedict XVI, Address to the New Ambassador of Guatemala, May 31, 2008.

ened by the rise in the price of agricultural products, new strategies need to be worked out in the fight against poverty and the promotion of rural development. This must also happen through structural-reform processes, that would enable the challenges of the same security and of climatic changes to be faced. Furthermore, it is necessary to increase the food available by promoting industrious small farmers and guaranteeing them access to the market. The global increase in the production of agricultural products, however, can be effective only if production is accompanied by effective distribution and if it is primarily destined to satisfy essential needs. It certainly is not easy, but it would allow, among other things, the rediscovery of the value of the rural family: it would not be limited to preserving the transmission, from parents to children, of the cultivation methods, of conserving and distributing foodstuffs, but above all it would preserve a model of life, of education, of culture, and of religiosity. Moreover, from the economic profile, it ensures an effective and loving attention to the weakest and, by virtue of the principle of subsidiarity, it could assume a direct role in the distribution chain and the trading of agricultural food products, reducing the costs of intermediaries and favoring small scale production.

Ladies and gentlemen,

Today's difficulties show how modern technology by itself is not sufficient to provide for the lack of food, neither are statistical calculations nor, in emergency situations, the sending of food supplies. All this certainly has a great impact, yet it must be completed and oriented to a political action that, inspired by those principles of the natural law which are written on the human heart, protect the dignity of the person. In this way also the order of creation is respected and one has "the good of all as a constant guiding criterion."[5] Hence, only by protecting the person is it possible to overcome the main causes of hunger, such as being closed to one's neighbor which dissolves solidarity, justifies models of consumerist life, and unravels the social fabric, preserving, if not actually deepening, the furrows of unjust balances and neglecting the most profound demands of good.[6] If, therefore, respect for human dignity were given its worth on the negotiation table, in making decisions and accomplishing them, it would be possible to rise above otherwise insurmountable obstacles and it would eliminate, or at least diminish, the lack of interest in the good of others. Consequently, it would be possible to adopt courageous measures that would not stop before hunger and malnutrition, as if they were simply considered unsolvable, endemic phenomena. It could help if, in the defense of human dignity, international action—even emergency action—were to estimate the superfluous in the perspective of the needs of others and to administer the fruit of creation according to justice, placing it at the disposition of all generations.

In the light of these principles, I hope that the delegations present at this meeting will take on new commitments and be resolved to accomplish them with great determination. The Catholic Church, for her part, desires to join in these efforts! In a spirit of collaboration, drawing on ancient wisdom, inspired by the Gospel, she makes a firm and heartfelt appeal that is very relevant for those participating in the summit: "Give food to the

---

5. Benedict XVI, Message for the 2008 World Day of Peace, n. 7, January 1, 2008.
6. Cf. Benedict XVI, Deus Caritas Est, n. 28.

one who is starving, because, if you do not give to him food, you will kill him."[7] I assure you that, along this path, you can count on the support of the Holy See. Although it differentiates itself from states, it is united to their most noble objectives to seal a commitment that, by her nature, involves the entire international community: to encourage every people to share the needs of other peoples, placing in common the goods of the earth that the Creator has destined for the entire human family.

### Selfishness and Speculation as Obstacles to the Fight against Hunger

From Message to Mr. Jacques Diouf, Director General
of FAO, on the Occasion of World Food Day 2008,
October 13, 2008

The theme chosen this year for Word Food Day, "World Food Security: the Challenges of Climate Change and Bioenergy," permits a reflection on what has been achieved in the fight against hunger and on the obstacles to the action of the Food and Agriculture Organization of the United Nations in the face of new challenges that threaten the life of the human family.

This day is being celebrated at a particularly difficult time for the world nutritional situation, when the availability of foods seems inadequate in relation to consumption, and climate change contributes to endangering the survival of millions of men, women, and children, forced to leave their country in

7. Cf. *Decretum Gratiani*, D. 86, c. 21.

search of food. These circumstances mean that, together with the FAO, everyone must respond in terms of solidarity with actions free from all conditions and truly at the service of the common good.

Last June, the High-Level Conference on Word Food Security afforded the FAO an opportunity to remind the international community of its direct responsibilities for food insecurity while basic aid for emergency situations risks being limited. In the message I addressed to the participants at the time I pointed out the need "to adopt courageous measures that would not stop before hunger and malnutrition, as if they simply concerned unsolvable, endemic phenomena."[8]

The first task is to eliminate the causes that prevent authentic respect for the person's dignity. The means and resources of which the world disposes today can procure sufficient food to satisfy the growing needs of all. This has been demonstrated by the first results of the effort to increase global production levels in the face of the shortage recorded in recent harvests. So why is it not possible to prevent so many people suffering the most extreme consequences of hunger? There are numerous reasons for this situation in which abundance and a deficit often coexist. Thus one can mention the food race that does not stop in spite of the constantly diminishing supply of foodstuffs which imposes reductions on the nutritional capacity of the poorest regions of the world, or the lack of determination to conclude negotiations and to check the selfishness of states and groups of coun-

8. Benedict XVI, Message to Participants Attending the High-Level Conference on World Food Security: The Challenges of Climate Change and Bioenergy, Organized by the United Nations Food and Agriculture Organization, June 2, 2008.

tries or further, to put an end to that "unbridled speculation" which affects the mechanisms of prices and consumption. The absence of a correct administration of food resources caused by corruption in public life or growing investments in weapons and sophisticated military technology to the detriment of the primary needs of people also plays an important role.

These very different reasons originate in a false sense of the values on which international relations should be based and, in particular, in the widespread attitude in contemporary culture which gives exclusive priority to the race for material goods, forgetting the true nature of the human person and his deepest aspirations. Unfortunately, the result is the inability of many to take charge of the needs of the poor and to understand them, and the denial of their inalienable dignity. An effective campaign against hunger thus demands far more than a mere scientific study to confront climate change or give priority to the agricultural production of food. It is necessary first of all to rediscover the meaning of the human person, in his individual and community dimensions, from the founding of family life, a source of love and affection from which the sense of solidarity and sharing develop. This setting satisfies the need to build relations between peoples, based on constant and authentic availability, to enable each country to satisfy the requirements of needy people but also to transmit the idea of relations based on a reciprocal exchange of knowledge, values, rapid assistance, and respect.

This commitment to promoting effective social justice in international relations demands of each one an awareness that the goods of creation are destined for all, and that in the world community economies must be oriented toward the sharing of these goods, their lasting use, and the fair division of the benefits that derive from them.

In the changing context of international relations, where uncertainties seem to be growing and new challenges are glimpsed, the experience acquired to date by the FAO alongside that of other institutions active in the fight against hunger can play a fundamental role in promoting a new way of understanding international cooperation. One essential condition for increasing production levels, for guaranteeing the identity of indigenous communities as well as peace and security in the world, is to guarantee access to land, thereby favoring farm workers and upholding their rights.

The Catholic Church is close to you in all these efforts. This is testified by the attention with which the Holy See has followed the activity of the FAO since 1948, constantly supporting your endeavors so that your commitment to the cause of the human being might be pursued. This means, in practice, openness to life, respect for the order of creation, and adherence to the ethical principles that have always been the basis of social life.

## Fighting Poverty to Build Peace

From Message for the Celebration of the
World Day of Peace, January 1, 2009

1. Once again, as the new year begins, I want to extend good wishes for peace to people everywhere. With this message I would like to propose a reflection on the theme: "Fighting Pover-

ty to Build Peace." Back in 1993, my venerable predecessor Pope John Paul II, in his Message for the World Day of Peace that year, drew attention to the negative repercussions for peace when entire populations live in poverty. Poverty is often a contributory factor or a compounding element in conflicts, including armed ones. In turn, these conflicts fuel further tragic situations of poverty. "Our world," he wrote, "shows increasing evidence of another grave threat to peace: many individuals and indeed whole peoples are living today in conditions of extreme poverty. The gap between rich and poor has become more marked, even in the most economically developed nations. This is a problem which the conscience of humanity cannot ignore, since the conditions in which a great number of people are living are an insult to their innate dignity and as a result are a threat to the authentic and harmonious progress of the world community."[9]

2. In this context, fighting poverty requires *attentive consideration of the complex phenomenon of globalization*. This is important from a methodological standpoint, because it suggests drawing upon the fruits of economic and sociological research into the many different aspects of poverty. Yet the reference to globalization should also alert us to the spiritual and moral implications of the question, urging us, in our dealings with the poor, to set out from the clear recognition that we all share in a single divine plan: we are called to form one family in which all—individuals, peoples, and nations—model their behavior according to the principles of fraternity and responsibility.

This perspective requires an understanding of poverty that is wide-ranging and well articulated. If it were a question of ma-

9. John Paul II, Message for the 1993 World Day of Peace, n. 1, January 1, 1993.

terial poverty alone, then the social sciences, which enable us to measure phenomena on the basis of mainly quantitative data, would be sufficient to illustrate its principal characteristics. Yet we know that other, non-material forms of poverty exist which are not the direct and automatic consequence of material deprivation. For example, in advanced wealthy societies, there is evidence of *marginalization,* as well as *affective, moral, and spiritual poverty,* seen in people whose interior lives are disoriented and who experience various forms of malaise despite their economic prosperity. On the one hand, I have in mind what is known as "moral underdevelopment,"[10] and on the other hand the negative consequences of "superdevelopment."[11] Nor can I forget that, in so-called "poor" societies, economic growth is often hampered by *cultural impediments* which lead to inefficient use of available resources. It remains true, however, that every form of externally imposed poverty has at its root a lack of respect for the transcendent dignity of the human person. When man is not considered within the total context of his vocation, and when the demands of a true "human ecology"[12] are not respected, the cruel forces of poverty are unleashed, as is evident in certain specific areas that I shall now consider briefly one by one.

## POVERTY AND MORAL IMPLICATIONS

3. Poverty is often considered a consequence of *demographic change.* For this reason, there are international campaigns afoot to reduce birthrates, sometimes using methods that respect neither the dignity of the woman, nor the right of parents to

10. Paul VI, Encyclical Letter *Populorum Progressio* (March 26, 1967), n. 19.

11. John Paul II, Encyclical Letter *Sollicitudo Rei Socialis* (December 30, 1987), n. 28.

12. John Paul II, *Centesimus Annus,* n. 38.

choose responsibly how many children to have;[13] graver still, these methods often fail to respect even the right to life. The extermination of millions of unborn children, in the name of the fight against poverty, actually constitutes the destruction of the poorest of all human beings. And yet it remains the case that in 1981, around 40 percent of the world's population was below the threshold of absolute poverty, while today that percentage has been reduced by as much as a half, and whole peoples have escaped from poverty despite experiencing substantial demographic growth. This goes to show that resources to solve the problem of poverty do exist, even in the face of an increasing population. Nor must it be forgotten that, since the end of the Second World War, the world's population has grown by four billion, largely because of certain countries that have recently emerged on the international scene as new economic powers, and have experienced rapid development specifically because of the large number of their inhabitants. Moreover, among the most developed nations, those with higher birthrates enjoy better opportunities for development. In other words, population is proving to be an asset, not a factor that contributes to poverty.

4. Another area of concern has to do with *pandemic diseases,* such as malaria, tuberculosis, and AIDS. Insofar as they affect the wealth-producing sectors of the population, they are a significant factor in the overall deterioration of conditions in the country concerned. Efforts to rein in the consequences of these diseases on the population do not always achieve significant results. It also happens that countries afflicted by some of these pandemics find themselves held hostage, when they try to address them, by

13. Cf. Paul VI, *Populorum Progressio,* n. 37; John Paul II, *Sollicitudo Rei Socialis,* n. 25.

those who make economic aid conditional upon the implementation of anti-life policies. It is especially hard to combat AIDS, a major cause of poverty, unless the moral issues connected with the spread of the virus are also addressed. First and foremost, educational campaigns are needed, aimed especially at the young, to promote a sexual ethic that fully corresponds to the dignity of the person; initiatives of this kind have already borne important fruits, causing a reduction in the spread of AIDS. Then, too, the necessary medicines and treatment must be made available to poorer peoples as well. This presupposes a determined effort to promote medical research and innovative forms of treatment, as well as flexible application, when required, of the international rules protecting intellectual property, so as to guarantee necessary basic healthcare to all people.

5. A third area requiring attention in programs for fighting poverty, which once again highlights its intrinsic moral dimension, is *child poverty*. When poverty strikes a family, the children prove to be the most vulnerable victims: almost half of those living in absolute poverty today are children. To take the side of children when considering poverty means giving priority to those objectives which concern them most directly, such as caring for mothers; commitment to education; access to vaccines, medical care, and drinking water; safeguarding the environment; and, above all, commitment to defense of the family and the stability of relations within it. When the family is weakened, it is inevitably children who suffer. If the dignity of women and mothers is not protected, it is the children who are affected most.

6. A fourth area needing particular attention from the moral standpoint is the *relationship between disarmament and develop-*

*ment.* The current level of world military expenditure gives cause for concern. As I have pointed out before, it can happen that "immense military expenditure, involving material and human resources and arms, is in fact diverted from development projects for peoples, especially the poorest who are most in need of aid. This is contrary to what is stated in the Charter of the United Nations, which engages the international community and states in particular 'to promote the establishment and maintenance of international peace and security with the least diversion for armaments of the world's human and economic resources.'"[14]

This state of affairs does nothing to promote, and indeed seriously impedes, attainment of the ambitious development targets of the international community. What is more, an excessive increase in military expenditure risks accelerating the arms race, producing pockets of underdevelopment and desperation, so that it can paradoxically become a cause of instability, tension, and conflict. As my venerable predecessor Paul VI wisely observed, "the new name for peace is development."[15] States are therefore invited to reflect seriously on the underlying reasons for conflicts, often provoked by injustice, and to practice courageous self-criticism. If relations can be improved, it should be possible to reduce expenditure on arms. The resources saved could then be earmarked for development projects to assist the poorest and most needy individuals and peoples: efforts expended in this way would be efforts for peace within the human family.

14. Benedict XVI, Letter to Cardinal Renato Raffaele Martino on the Occasion of the International Seminar Organized by the Pontifical Council for Justice and Peace on the Theme: "Disarmament, Development, and Peace. Prospects for Integral Disarmament," April 10, 2008.

15. Paul VI, *Populorum Progressio*, n. 87.

7. A fifth area connected with the fight against material poverty concerns the *current food crisis,* which places in jeopardy the fulfillment of basic needs. This crisis is characterized not so much by a shortage of food, as by difficulty in gaining access to it and by different forms of speculation: in other words, by a structural lack of political and economic institutions capable of addressing needs and emergencies. Malnutrition can also cause grave mental and physical damage to the population, depriving many people of the energy necessary to escape from poverty unaided. This contributes to the widening gap of inequality, and can provoke violent reactions. All the indicators of relative poverty in recent years point to an increased disparity between rich and poor. No doubt the principal reasons for this are, on the one hand, advances in technology, which mainly benefit the more affluent, and on the other hand, changes in the prices of industrial products, which rise much faster than those of agricultural products and raw materials in the possession of poorer countries. In this way, the majority of the population in the poorest countries suffers a double marginalization, through the adverse effects of lower incomes and higher prices.

## GLOBAL SOLIDARITY AND THE
## FIGHT AGAINST POVERTY

8. One of the most important ways of building peace is through a form of globalization directed toward the interests of the whole human family.[16] In order to govern globalization, however, there needs to be a strong sense of *global solidarity* be-

16. Cf. John Paul II, *Centesimus Annus,* n. 58.

tween rich and poor countries,[17] as well as within individual countries, including affluent ones. A "common code of ethics"[18] is also needed, consisting of norms based not upon mere consensus, but rooted in the natural law inscribed by the Creator on the conscience of every human being (cf. Rom 2:14–15). Does not every one of us sense deep within his or her conscience a call to make a personal contribution to the common good and to peace in society? Globalization eliminates certain barriers, but is still able to build new ones; it brings peoples together, but spatial and temporal proximity does not of itself create the conditions for true communion and authentic peace. Effective means to redress the marginalization of the world's poor through globalization will only be found if people everywhere feel personally outraged by the injustices in the world and by the concomitant violations of human rights. The Church, which is the "sign and instrument of communion with God and of the unity of the entire human race,"[19] will continue to offer her contribution so that injustices and misunderstandings may be resolved, leading to a world of greater peace and solidarity.

9. In the field of *international commerce* and *finance,* there are processes at work today which permit a positive integration of economies, leading to an overall improvement in conditions, but there are also processes tending in the opposite direction, dividing and marginalizing peoples, and creating dangerous

17. Cf. John Paul II, Address to the Members of the Italian Christian Workers' Associations, n. 4, April 27, 2002.

18. John Paul II, Address to the Plenary Assembly of the Pontifical Academy of Social Sciences, n. 4, April 27, 2001.

19. Second Vatican Council, Dogmatic Constitution *Lumen Gentium* (November 21, 1964), n. 1.

situations that can erupt into wars and conflicts. Since the Second World War, international trade in goods and services has grown extraordinarily fast, with a momentum unprecedented in history. Much of this global trade has involved countries that were industrialized early, with the significant addition of many newly emerging countries which have now entered onto the world stage. Yet there are other low-income countries which are still seriously marginalized in terms of trade. Their growth has been negatively influenced by the rapid decline, seen in recent decades, in the prices of commodities, which constitute practically the whole of their exports. In these countries, which are mostly in Africa, dependence on the exportation of commodities continues to constitute a potent risk factor. Here I should like to renew an appeal for all countries to be given equal opportunities of access to the world market, without exclusion or marginalization.

10. A similar reflection may be made in the area of finance, which is a key aspect of the phenomenon of globalization, owing to the development of technology and policies of liberalization in the flow of capital between countries. Objectively, the most important function of finance is to sustain the possibility of long-term investment and hence of development. Today this appears extremely fragile: it is experiencing the negative repercussions of a system of financial dealings—both national and global—based upon very short-term thinking, which aims at increasing the value of financial operations and concentrates on the technical management of various forms of risk. The recent crisis demonstrates how financial activity can at times be completely turned in on itself, lacking any long-term consideration

of the common good. This lowering of the objectives of global finance to the very short term reduces its capacity to function as a bridge between the present and the future, and as a stimulus to the creation of new opportunities for production and for work in the long term. Finance limited in this way to the short and very short term becomes dangerous for everyone, even for those who benefit when the markets perform well.[20]

11. All of this would indicate that the fight against poverty requires cooperation both on the economic level and on the legal level, so as to allow the international community, and especially poorer countries, to identify and implement coordinated strategies to deal with the problems discussed above, thereby providing an effective legal framework for the economy. Incentives are needed for establishing efficient participatory institutions, and support is needed in fighting crime and fostering a culture of legality. On the other hand, it cannot be denied that policies which place too much emphasis on assistance underlie many of the failures in providing aid to poor countries. Investing in the formation of people and developing a specific and well-integrated culture of enterprise would seem at present to be the right approach in the medium and long term. If economic activities require a favorable context in order to develop, this must not distract attention from the need to generate revenue. While it has been rightly emphasized that increasing per capita income cannot be the ultimate goal of political and economic activity, it is still an important means of attaining the objective of the fight against hunger and absolute poverty. Hence, the illusion

20. Cf. *Compendium of the Social Doctrine of the Church* (2004), n. 368.

that a policy of mere redistribution of existing wealth can definitively resolve the problem must be set aside. In a modern economy, the value of assets is utterly dependent on the capacity to generate revenue in the present and the future. Wealth creation therefore becomes an inescapable duty, which must be kept in mind if the fight against material poverty is to be effective in the long term.

12. If the poor are to be given priority, then there has to be enough room for *an ethical approach to economics* on the part of those active in the international market, *an ethical approach to politics* on the part of those in public office, and an *ethical approach to participation* capable of harnessing the contributions of civil society at local and international levels. International agencies themselves have come to recognize the value and advantage of economic initiatives taken by civil society or local administrations to promote the emancipation and social inclusion of those sectors of the population that often fall below the threshold of extreme poverty and yet are not easily reached by official aid. The history of twentieth-century economic development teaches us that good development policies depend for their effectiveness on responsible implementation by human agents and on the creation of positive partnerships between markets, civil society, and states. Civil society in particular plays a key part in every process of development, since development is essentially a cultural phenomenon, and culture is born and develops in the civil sphere.[21]

13. As my venerable predecessor Pope John Paul II had occasion to remark, globalization "is notably ambivalent" and

21. Cf. ibid., n. 356.

therefore needs to be managed with great prudence.[22] This will include giving priority to the needs of the world's poor, and overcoming the scandal of the imbalance between the problems of poverty and the measures which have been adopted in order to address them. The imbalance lies both in the cultural and political order and in the spiritual and moral order. In fact we often consider only the superficial and instrumental causes of poverty without attending to those harbored within the human heart, like greed and narrow vision. The problems of development, aid, and international cooperation are sometimes addressed without any real attention to the human element, but as merely technical questions—limited, that is, to establishing structures, setting up trade agreements, and allocating funding impersonally. What the fight against poverty really needs are men and women who live in a profoundly fraternal way and are able to accompany individuals, families, and communities on journeys of authentic human development.

## CONCLUSION

14. In the encyclical letter *Centesimus Annus,* John Paul II warned of the need to "abandon a mentality in which the poor—as individuals and as peoples—are considered a burden, as irksome intruders trying to consume what others have produced." The poor, he wrote, "ask for the right to share in enjoying material goods and to make good use of their capacity for work, thus creating a world that is more just and prosperous for all."[23]

---

22. John Paul II, Address to Leaders of Trade Unions and Workers' Associations, n. 3, May 2, 2000.

23. John Paul II, *Centesimus Annus*, n. 28.

In today's globalized world, it is increasingly evident that peace can be built only if everyone is assured the possibility of reasonable growth: sooner or later, the distortions produced by unjust systems have to be paid for by everyone. It is utterly foolish to build a luxury home in the midst of desert or decay. Globalization on its own is incapable of building peace, and in many cases, it actually creates divisions and conflicts. If anything it points to a need: to be oriented toward a goal of profound solidarity that seeks the good of each and all. In this sense, globalization should be seen as a good opportunity to achieve something important in the fight against poverty, and to place at the disposal of justice and peace resources which were scarcely conceivable previously.

15. The Church's social teaching has always been concerned with the poor. At the time of the encyclical letter *Rerum Novarum,* the poor were identified mainly as the workers in the new industrial society; in the social magisterium of Pius XI, Pius XII, John XXIII, Paul VI, and John Paul II, new forms of poverty were gradually explored, as the scope of the social question widened to reach global proportions.[24] This expansion of the social question to the worldwide scale has to be considered not just as a quantitative extension, but also as a qualitative growth in the understanding of man and the needs of the human family. For this reason, while attentively following the current phenomena of globalization and their impact on human poverty, the Church points out the new aspects of the social question, not only in their breadth but also in their depth, insofar as they concern man's identity and his relationship with God. These principles

24. Cf. Paul VI, *Populorum Progressio,* n. 3.

of social teaching tend to clarify the links between poverty and globalization and they help to guide action toward the building of peace. Among these principles, it is timely to recall in particular the "preferential love for the poor,"[25] in the light of the primacy of charity, which is attested throughout Christian tradition, beginning with that of the early Church (cf. Acts 4:32–36; 1 Cor 16:1; 2 Cor 8–9; Gal 2:10).

"Everyone should put his hand to the work which falls to his share, at once and immediately," wrote Leo XIII in 1891, and he added: "In regard to the Church, her cooperation will never be wanting, be the time or the occasion what it may."[26] It is in the same spirit that the Church to this day carries out her work for the poor, in whom she sees Christ,[27] and she constantly hears echoing in her heart the command of the Prince of Peace to his Apostles: *"Vos date illis manducare*—Give them something to eat yourselves" (Lk 9:13). Faithful to this summons from the Lord, the Christian community will never fail, then, to assure the entire human family of her support through gestures of creative solidarity, not only by "giving from one's surplus," but above all by "a change of lifestyles, of models of production and consumption, and of the established structures of power which today govern societies."[28] At the start of the New Year, then, I extend to every disciple of Christ and to every person of good will a warm invitation to expand their hearts to meet the needs of the poor and to take whatever practical steps are possible in

25. John Paul II, *Sollicitudo Rei Socialis*, n. 42; cf. John Paul II, *Centesimus Annus*, n. 57.

26. Leo XIII, Encyclical Letter *Rerum Novarum* (May 15, 1891), n. 45.

27. Cf. John Paul II, *Centesimus Annus*, n. 58.

28. Ibid.

order to help them. The truth of the axiom cannot be refuted: "to fight poverty is to build peace."

## *An Equitable Access to the Earth's Resources Should Be Guaranteed to Everyone*

From Address to Participants in the Thirty-first Session of the Governing Council of the International Fund for Agricultural Development (IFAD), February 20, 2009

I am pleased to have this opportunity to meet all of you at the conclusion of the celebrations marking the thirtieth anniversary of the establishment of the International Fund for Agricultural Development. I thank the outgoing president, Mr. Lennart Båge, for his kind words and I offer congratulations and good wishes to Mr. Kanayo Nwanze on his election to this high office. I thank all of you for coming here today and I assure you of my prayers for the important work that you do to promote rural development. Your work is particularly crucial at the present time in view of the damaging effect on food security of the current instability in the prices of agricultural products. This requires new and far-sighted strategies for the fight against rural poverty and the promotion of rural development. As you know, the Holy See fully shares your commitment to overcome poverty and hunger, and to come to the aid of the world's poorest peoples. I pray that IFAD's anniversary celebration will provide you with an incentive to pursue these worthy goals with renewed energy and determination in the years ahead.

Since its earliest days, the International Fund has achieved an exemplary form of cooperation and co-responsibility between nations at different stages of development. When wealthy countries and developing nations come together to make joint decisions and to determine specific criteria for each country's budgetary contribution to the fund, it can truly be said that the various member states come together as equals, expressing their solidarity with one another and their shared commitment to eradicate poverty and hunger. In an increasingly interdependent world, joint decision-making processes of this kind are essential if international affairs are to be conducted with equity and foresight.

Equally commendable is the emphasis placed by IFAD on promoting employment opportunities within rural communities, with a view to enabling them, in the long term, to become independent of outside aid. Assistance given to local producers serves to build up the economy and contributes to the overall development of the nation concerned. In this sense the "rural credit" projects, designed to assist smallholder farmers and agricultural workers with no land of their own, can boost the wider economy and provide greater food security for all. These projects also help indigenous communities to flourish on their own soil, and to live in harmony with their traditional culture, instead of being forced to uproot themselves in order to seek employment in overcrowded cities, teeming with social problems, where they often have to endure squalid living conditions.

This approach has the particular merit of restoring the agricultural sector to its rightful place within the economy and the social fabric of developing nations. Here a valuable contribution can be made by non-governmental organizations, some of which have close links with the Catholic Church and are committed to the application of her social teaching. The principle of subsidiarity requires that each group within society be free to make its proper contribution to the good of the whole. All too often, agricultural workers in developing nations are denied that opportunity, when their labor is greedily exploited, and their produce is diverted to distant markets, with little or no resulting benefit for the local community itself.

Almost fifty years ago, my predecessor Blessed Pope John XXIII had this to say about the task of tilling the soil: "Those who live on the land can hardly fail to appreciate the nobility of the work they are called upon to do. They are living in close harmony with Nature—the majestic temple of Creation.... Theirs is a work which carries with it a dignity all its own."[29] All human labor is a participation in the creative providence of Almighty God, but agricultural labor is so in a pre-eminent way. A truly humane society will always know how to appreciate and reward appropriately the contribution made by the agricultural sector. If properly supported and equipped, it has the potential to lift a nation out of poverty and to lay the foundations for increasing prosperity.

Ladies and gentlemen, as we give thanks for the achievements of the past thirty years, there is a need for renewed determination to act in harmony and solidarity with all the different elements of the human family in order to ensure equitable access to the earth's resources now and in the future. The motivation to do this comes from love: love for the poor, love that cannot tolerate injustice or deprivation, love that refuses to rest until poverty and hunger are banished from our midst. The

29. John XXIII, Encyclical Letter *Mater et Magistra* (May 15, 1961), nn.144–45.

goals of eradicating extreme poverty and hunger, as well as promoting food security and rural development, far from being over-ambitious or unrealistic, become, in this context, imperatives binding upon the whole international community. It is my fervent prayer that the activities of such organizations as yours will continue to make a significant contribution to the attainment of these goals. In thanking you and encouraging you to persevere in the good work that you do, I commend you to the constant care of our loving Father, the Creator of heaven and earth and all that is therein. May God bless all of you!

## Integral Human Development in Charity and in Truth

From Encyclical Letter *Caritas in Veritate* to the Bishops, Priests, and Deacons, Religious Men and Women, the Lay Faithful, and All People of Good Will on Integral Human Development in Charity and Truth, June 29, 2009

### HUMAN DEVELOPMENT IN OUR TIME

27. Life in many poor countries is still extremely insecure as a consequence of food shortages, and the situation could become worse: *hunger* still reaps enormous numbers of victims among those who, like Lazarus, are not permitted to take their place at the rich man's table, contrary to the hopes expressed by Paul VI.[30] *Feed the hungry* (cf. Mt 25:35, 37, 42) is an ethical imperative for the universal Church, as she responds to the teachings of her Founder, the Lord Jesus, concerning solidarity and the

30. Paul VI, *Populorum Progressio*, n. 4; cf. John Paul II, *Sollicitudo Rei Socialis*, n. 42.

sharing of goods. Moreover, the elimination of world hunger has also, in the global era, become a requirement for safeguarding the peace and stability of the planet. Hunger is not so much dependent on lack of material things as on shortage of social resources, the most important of which are institutional. What is missing, in other words, is a network of economic institutions capable of guaranteeing regular access to sufficient food and water for nutritional needs, and also capable of addressing the primary needs and necessities ensuing from genuine food crises, whether due to natural causes or political irresponsibility, nationally and internationally. The problem of food insecurity needs to be addressed within a long-term perspective, eliminating the structural causes that give rise to it and promoting the agricultural development of poorer countries. This can be done by investing in rural infrastructures, irrigation systems, transport, organization of markets, and in the development and dissemination of agricultural technology that can make the best use of the human, natural, and socio-economic resources that are more readily available at the local level, while guaranteeing their sustainability over the long term as well. All this needs to be accomplished with the involvement of local communities in choices and decisions that affect the use of agricultural land. In this perspective, it could be useful to consider the new possibilities that are opening up through proper use of traditional as well as innovative farming techniques, always assuming that these have been judged, after sufficient testing, to be appropriate, respectful of the environment, and attentive to the needs of the most deprived peoples. At the same time, the question of equitable agrarian reform in developing countries should not be ignored. The right to food, like the right to water, has an important place within the pursuit of other rights, beginning with the fundamental right to life. It is therefore necessary to cultivate a public conscience that considers *food and access to water as universal rights of all human beings, without distinction or discrimination*.[31] It is important, moreover, to emphasize that solidarity with poor countries in the process of development can point toward a solution of the current global crisis, as politicians and directors of international institutions have begun to sense in recent times. Through support for economically poor countries by means of financial plans inspired by solidarity—so that these countries can take steps to satisfy their own citizens' demand for consumer goods and for development—not only can true economic growth be generated, but a contribution can be made toward sustaining the productive capacities of rich countries that risk being compromised by the crisis.

40. Today's international economic scene, marked by grave deviations and failures, requires a *profoundly new way of understanding business enterprise*. Old models are disappearing, but promising new ones are taking shape on the horizon. Without doubt, one of the greatest risks for businesses is that they are almost exclusively answerable to their investors, thereby limiting their social value. Owing to their growth in scale and the need for more and more capital, it is becoming increasingly rare for business enterprises to be in the hands of a stable director who feels responsible in the long term, not just the short term, for the life and the results of his company, and it is becoming

31. Cf. Benedict XVI, Message for the 2007 World Food Day, nn. 33–35, October 4, 2007.

increasingly rare for businesses to depend on a single territory. Moreover, the so-called outsourcing of production can weaken the company's sense of responsibility toward the stakeholders— namely the workers, the suppliers, the consumers, the natural environment, and broader society—in favor of the shareholders, who are not tied to a specific geographical area and who therefore enjoy extraordinary mobility. Today's international capital market offers great freedom of action. Yet there is also increasing awareness of the need for greater *social responsibility* on the part of business. Even if the ethical considerations that currently inform debate on the social responsibility of the corporate world are not all acceptable from the perspective of the Church's social doctrine, there is nevertheless a growing conviction that *business management cannot concern itself only with the interests of the proprietors, but must also assume responsibility for all the other stakeholders who contribute to the life of the business:* the workers, the clients, the suppliers of various elements of production, the community of reference. In recent years a new cosmopolitan class of *managers* has emerged, who are often answerable only to the shareholders, generally consisting of anonymous funds which de facto determine their remuneration. By contrast, though, many far-sighted managers today are becoming increasingly aware of the profound links between their enterprise and the territory or territories in which it operates. Paul VI invited people to give serious attention to the damage that can be caused to one's home country by the transfer abroad of capital purely for personal advantage.[32] John Paul II taught that *investment always has moral, as well as economic significance.*[33] All this—it should be stressed—is

32. Cf. ibid., n. 24.                    33. John Paul II, *Centesimus Annus*, n. 36.

still valid today, despite the fact that the capital market has been significantly liberalized, and modern technological thinking can suggest that investment is merely a technical act, not a human and ethical one. There is no reason to deny that a certain amount of capital can do good, if invested abroad rather than at home. Yet the requirements of justice must be safeguarded, with due consideration for the way in which the capital was generated and the harm to individuals that will result if it is not used where it was produced.[34] What should be avoided is a speculative *use of financial resources* that yields to the temptation of seeking only short-term profit, without regard for the long-term sustainability of the enterprise, its benefit to the real economy, and attention to the advancement, in suitable and appropriate ways, of further economic initiatives in countries in need of development. It is true that the export of investments and skills can benefit the populations of the receiving country. Labor and technical knowledge are universal goods. Yet it is not right to export these things merely for the sake of obtaining advantageous conditions, or worse, for purposes of exploitation, without making a real contribution to local society by helping to bring about a robust productive and social system, an essential factor for stable development.

## DEVELOPMENT OF PEOPLES, RIGHTS AND DUTIES, THE ENVIRONMENT

48. Today the subject of development is also closely related to the duties arising from *our relationship to the natural environ-*

---

34. Cf. Paul VI, *Populorum Progressio*, n. 24.

*ment.* The environment is God's gift to everyone, and in our use of it we have a responsibility toward the poor, toward future generations, and toward humanity as a whole. When nature, including the human being, is viewed as the result of mere chance or evolutionary determinism, our sense of responsibility wanes. In nature, the believer recognizes the wonderful result of God's creative activity, which we may use responsibly to satisfy our legitimate needs, material or otherwise, while respecting the intrinsic balance of creation. If this vision is lost, we end up either considering nature an untouchable taboo or, on the contrary, abusing it. Neither attitude is consonant with the Christian vision of nature as the fruit of God's creation.

*Nature expresses a design of love and truth.* It is prior to us, and it has been given to us by God as the setting for our life. Nature speaks to us of the Creator (cf. Rom 1:20) and his love for humanity. It is destined to be "recapitulated" in Christ at the end of time (cf. Eph 1:9–10; Col 1:19–20). Thus it too is a "vocation."[35] Nature is at our disposal not as "a heap of scattered refuse,"[36] but as a gift of the Creator who has given it an inbuilt order, enabling man to draw from it the principles needed in order "to till it and keep it" (Gn 2:15). But it should also be stressed that it is contrary to authentic development to view nature as something more important than the human person. This position leads to attitudes of neopaganism or a new pantheism—human salvation cannot come from nature alone, understood in a purely naturalistic sense. This having been said, it is also necessary to reject the

35. John Paul II, Message for the 1990 World Day of Peace, n. 6, January 1, 1990.

36. Heraclitus of Ephesus, Fragment 22B124, in Hermann Diels and Walther Kranz, *Die Fragmente der Vorsokratiker,* 6th ed. (Berlin: Weidmann, 1952).

opposite position, which aims at total technical dominion over nature, because the natural environment is more than raw material to be manipulated at our pleasure; it is a wondrous work of the Creator containing a "grammar" which sets forth ends and criteria for its wise use, not its reckless exploitation. Today much harm is done to development precisely as a result of these distorted notions. Reducing nature merely to a collection of contingent data ends up doing violence to the environment and even encouraging activity that fails to respect human nature itself. Our nature, constituted not only by matter but also by spirit, and as such, endowed with transcendent meaning and aspirations, is also normative for culture. Human beings interpret and shape the natural environment through culture, which in turn is given direction by the responsible use of freedom, in accordance with the dictates of the moral law. Consequently, projects for integral human development cannot ignore coming generations, but need to be *marked by solidarity and intergenerational justice,* while taking into account a variety of contexts: ecological, juridical, economic, political, and cultural.[37]

49. Questions linked to the care and preservation of the environment today need to give due consideration to *the energy problem.* The fact that some states, power groups, and companies hoard non-renewable energy resources represents a grave obstacle to development in poor countries. Those countries lack the economic means either to gain access to existing sources of non-renewable energy or to finance research into new alternatives. The stockpiling of natural resources, which in many

37. *Compendium of the Social Doctrine of the Church,* nn. 451–87.

cases are found in the poor countries themselves, gives rise to exploitation and frequent conflicts between and within nations. These conflicts are often fought on the soil of those same countries, with a heavy toll of death, destruction, and further decay. The international community has an urgent duty to find institutional means of regulating the exploitation of non-renewable resources, involving poor countries in the process, in order to plan together for the future.

On this front too, there is a *pressing moral need for renewed solidarity,* especially in relationships between developing countries and those that are highly industrialized.[38] The technologically advanced societies can and must lower their domestic energy consumption, either through an evolution in manufacturing methods or through greater ecological sensitivity among their citizens. It should be added that at present it is possible to achieve improved energy efficiency while at the same time encouraging research into alternative forms of energy. What is also needed, though, is a worldwide redistribution of energy resources, so that countries lacking those resources can have access to them. The fate of those countries cannot be left in the hands of whoever is first to claim the spoils, or whoever is able to prevail over the rest. Here we are dealing with major issues; if they are to be faced adequately, then everyone must responsibly recognize the impact they will have on future generations, particularly on the many young people in the poorer nations, who "ask to assume their active part in the construction of a better world."[39]

---

38. Cf. John Paul II, Message for the 1990 World Day of Peace, n. 10, January 1, 1990.
39. Paul VI, *Populorum Progressio,* n. 65.

50. This responsibility is a global one, for it is concerned not just with energy but with the whole of creation, which must not be bequeathed to future generations depleted of its resources. Human beings legitimately exercise a *responsible stewardship over nature,* in order to protect it, to enjoy its fruits, and to cultivate it in new ways, with the assistance of advanced technologies, so that it can worthily accommodate and feed the world's population. On this earth there is room for everyone: here the entire human family must find the resources to live with dignity, through the help of nature itself—God's gift to his children—and through hard work and creativity. At the same time we must recognize our grave duty to hand the earth on to future generations in such a condition that they too can worthily inhabit it and continue to cultivate it. This means being committed to making joint decisions "after pondering responsibly the road to be taken, decisions aimed at strengthening that *covenant between human beings and the environment,* which should mirror the creative love of God, from whom we come and toward whom we are journeying."[40] Let us hope that the international community and individual governments will succeed in countering harmful ways of treating the environment. It is likewise incumbent upon the competent authorities to make every effort to ensure that the economic and social costs of using up shared environmental resources are recognized with transparency and fully borne by those who incur them, not by other peoples or future generations: the protection of the environment, of resources, and of the climate obliges all international leaders to act jointly and to show a readiness to work in good faith, respecting

40. Benedict XVI, Message for the 2008 World Day of Peace, n. 7, January 1, 2008.

the law and promoting solidarity with the weakest regions of the planet.[41] One of the greatest challenges facing the economy is to achieve the most efficient use—not abuse—of natural resources, based on a realization that the notion of "efficiency" is not value-free.

51. *The way humanity treats the environment influences the way it treats itself, and vice versa.* This invites contemporary society to a serious review of its lifestyle, which, in many parts of the world, is prone to hedonism and consumerism, regardless of their harmful consequences.[42] What is needed is an effective shift in mentality which can lead to the adoption of *new lifestyles* "in which the quest for truth, beauty, goodness, and communion with others for the sake of common growth are the factors which determine consumer choices, savings, and investments."[43] Every violation of solidarity and civic friendship harms the environment, just as environmental deterioration in turn upsets relations in society. Nature, especially in our time, is so integrated into the dynamics of society and culture that by now it hardly constitutes an independent variable. Desertification and the decline in productivity in some agricultural areas are also the result of impoverishment and underdevelopment among their inhabitants. When incentives are offered for their economic and cultural development, nature itself is protected. Moreover, how many natural resources are squandered by wars! Peace in and among peoples would also provide greater protection for nature.

41. Cf. Benedict XVI, Address to the General Assembly of the United Nations Organization, Apostolic Journey to the United States of America, New York, April 18, 2008.

42. Cf. John Paul II, Message for the 1990 World Day of Peace, n. 13, January 1, 1990.

43. John Paul II, *Centesimus Annus*, n. 36.

The hoarding of resources, especially water, can generate serious conflicts among the peoples involved. Peaceful agreement about the use of resources can protect nature and, at the same time, the well-being of the societies concerned.

*The Church has a responsibility toward creation* and she must assert this responsibility in the public sphere. In so doing, she must defend not only earth, water, and air as gifts of creation that belong to everyone. She must above all protect mankind from self-destruction. There is need for what might be called a human ecology, correctly understood. The deterioration of nature is in fact closely connected to the culture that shapes human coexistence: *when "human ecology" is respected within society, environmental ecology also benefits.*[44] Just as human virtues are interrelated, such that the weakening of one places others at risk, so the ecological system is based on respect for a plan that affects both the health of society and its good relationship with nature.

In order to protect nature, it is not enough to intervene with economic incentives or deterrents; not even an opposite education is sufficient. These are important steps, but *the decisive issue is the overall moral tenor of society.* If there is a lack of respect for the right to life and to a natural death, if human conception, gestation, and birth are made artificial, if human embryos are sacrificed to research, the conscience of society ends up losing the concept of human ecology and, along with it, that of environmental ecology. It is contradictory to insist that future generations respect the natural environment when our educational

---

44. John Paul II, *Centesimus Annus,* n. 38; Benedict XVI, Message for the 2007 World Day of Peace, n. 8, January 1, 2007.

systems and laws do not help them to respect themselves. The book of nature is one and indivisible: it takes in not only the environment but also life, sexuality, marriage, the family, social relations: in a word, integral human development. Our duties toward the environment are linked to our duties toward the human person, considered in himself and in relation to others. It would be wrong to uphold one set of duties while trampling on the other. Herein lies a grave contradiction in our mentality and practice today: one which demeans the person, disrupts the environment, and damages society.

52. Truth, and the love which it reveals, cannot be produced: they can only be received as a gift. Their ultimate source is not, and cannot be, mankind, but only God, who is himself Truth and Love. This principle is extremely important for society and for development, since neither can be a purely human product; the vocation to development on the part of individuals and peoples is not based simply on human choice, but is an intrinsic part of a plan that is prior to us and constitutes for all of us a duty to be freely accepted. That which is prior to us and constitutes us—subsistent Love and Truth—shows us what goodness is, and in what our true happiness consists. *It shows us the road to true development.*

## THE DEVELOPMENT OF PEOPLES
## AND TECHNOLOGY

69. The challenge of development today is closely linked to *technological progress,* with its astounding applications in the field of biology. Technology—it is worth emphasizing—is a profoundly human reality, linked to the autonomy and freedom of man. In technology we express and confirm the hegemony of

the spirit over matter. "The human spirit, 'increasingly free of its bondage to creatures, can be more easily drawn to the worship and contemplation of the Creator.'"[45] Technology enables us to exercise dominion over matter, to reduce risks, to save labor, to improve our conditions of life. It touches the heart of the vocation of human labor: in technology, seen as the product of his genius, man recognizes himself and forges his own humanity. Technology is the objective side of human action[46] whose origin and raison d'être is found in the subjective element: the worker himself. For this reason, technology is never merely technology. It reveals man and his aspirations toward development, it expresses the inner tension that impels him gradually to overcome material limitations. *Technology, in this sense, is a response to God's command to till and to keep the land* (cf. Gn 2:15) that he has entrusted to humanity, and it must serve to reinforce the covenant between human beings and the environment, a covenant that should mirror God's creative love.

## *An Integral Human Development to Give Voice to Every Nation*

From Letter to Hon. Mr. Silvio Berlusconi, Prime Minister of
Italy, on the Occasion of the G8 Summit, July 1, 2009

With a view to the upcoming G8, the group of the heads of state and government of the most industrialized countries, that

45. Paul VI, *Populorum Progressio*, n. 41; cf. Second Vatican Council, *Gaudium et Spes*, n. 57.

46. Cf. John Paul II, Encyclical Letter *Laborem Exercens* (September 14, 1981), n. 5.

will be taking place in L'Aquila from 8 to 10 July under the Italian presidency, I am pleased to send a cordial greeting to you and to all the participants. I therefore willingly take the opportunity to make a contribution to the reflection on the meeting's themes, as I have done in the past. I was informed by my collaborators of the commitment with which the government, over which you have the honor to preside, is preparing for this important meeting. I am also aware of the attention you have given to the reflections which, based on the themes of the upcoming summit, have been formulated by the Holy See, the Catholic Church in Italy, and the Catholic world in general, as well as the representatives of other religions.

The participation of heads of state or government not only of the G8 but also of many other nations will ensure that in order to find ways to a shared solution to the principal problems that are affecting the economy, peace, and international security, the decisions to be adopted can more faithfully mirror the viewpoints and expectations of the peoples of all the continents. Broadened to encompass the discussions of the forthcoming summit, this participation therefore seems particularly timely, given the many problems in the world today that are highly interconnected and interdependent. I refer in particular to the challenges of the current economic and financial crisis, as well as to the disturbing data of the phenomenon of climate change. These cannot but impel us to wise discernment and new projects to "'convert' the model of global development,"[47] rendering it capable of effectively promoting integral human develop-

47. Benedict XVI, Angelus, November 12, 2006.

ment, inspired by the values of human solidarity and of charity in truth. Several of these themes are also treated in my third encyclical, *Caritas in Veritate,* which in the next few days will be released to the press.

In preparation for the Great Jubilee of the Year 2000, on the initiative of John Paul II, the Holy See paid great attention to the work of the G8. My venerable predecessor was in fact convinced that the liberation of the poorest countries from the burden of debt and, more generally, the uprooting of the causes of extreme poverty in the world depended on the full assumption of shared responsibility toward all humanity, which is incumbent on the most financially developed governments and states. These responsibilities have not diminished; on the contrary, they are even more urgent today. In the recent past partly thanks to the impetus that the Great Jubilee of 2000 gave to the search for adequate solutions to problems related to the debt and to the economic vulnerability of Africa and other poor countries, and partly thanks to the notable economic and political changes in the global scene the majority of less developed countries have been able to enjoy a period of extraordinary growth. This has permitted many of them to hope in the achievement of the goal fixed by the international community on the threshold of the third millennium: to defeat extreme poverty by 2015. Unfortunately, the financial and economic crisis that has been besieging the entire planet since the beginning of 2008 has transformed the circumstances. Now, there is a real risk not only that hopes of emerging from extreme poverty will be extinguished but on the contrary that even populations which have until now benefited from a minimum of material well-being will sink into poverty.

Furthermore, the current global economic crisis carries the threat of the cancellation or drastic reduction of programs for international aid, especially for Africa and for the other economically less developed countries. Therefore with the same force as that with which John Paul II asked for the cancellation of the foreign debt I too would like to appeal to the member countries of the G8, to the other states represented, and to the governments of the whole world to maintain and reinforce aid for development, especially aid destined to "make the most" of "human resources," not only in spite of the crisis, but precisely because it is one of the principal paths to its solution. Is it not in fact through investment in the human being in all the men and women of the earth that it will be possible to succeed in effectively dispelling the disturbing prospect of global recession? Is not this truly the way to obtain, to the extent possible, a trend in the world economy that benefits the inhabitants of every country, rich and poor, large and small?

The issue of access to education is intimately connected to the efficacy of international cooperation. Thus if it is true that "investing" in men and women is necessary, then the goal of basic education for all, without exception, by 2015 must not only be met but must also be generously reinforced. Education is an indispensable condition for democracy to function, for fighting corruption, for exercising political, economic, and social rights and for the effective recovery of all states, poor and rich alike. And, by correctly applying the principle of subsidiarity, the support of development cannot but take into account the far-reaching educational action that the Catholic Church and other religious denominations carry out in the world's poorest and most neglected regions.

I am therefore keen to remind the distinguished participants of the G8 that the measure of technical efficacy of the provisions to adopt in order to emerge from the crisis coincides with the measure of its ethical value. In other words, it is necessary to bear in mind practical human and family needs. I refer, for example, to the effective creation of positions for all, that enable workers to provide fittingly for their family's needs and to fulfill their primary responsibility as educators of their children and protagonists in the community to which they belong. "A society in which this right is systematically denied," John Paul II wrote, "in which economic policies do not allow workers to reach satisfactory levels of employment, cannot be justified from an ethical point of view, nor can that society attain social peace."[48] And for this very purpose the urgent need for a fair system of international trade is essential, putting into practice and if necessary even going beyond the decisions made in Doha in 2001 to promote development. I hope that all creative energy will be devoted to achieving the U.N. Millennium Goals concerning the elimination of extreme poverty by 2015. It is only right to reform the international financial structure to ensure effective coordination of national policies, to prevent credit speculation, and to guarantee a broad international availability of public and private credit at the service of production and work, especially in the neediest countries and regions.

The ethical legitimization of the political commitments of the G8 will naturally demand that they be confronted with the thought and needs of the entire international community.

---

48. John Paul II, *Centesimus Annus*, n. 43; cf., John Paul II, *Laborem Excercens*, n. 18.

To this end, it seems important to reinforce multilateralism, not only for economic matters but also for the entire spectrum of the issues concerning peace, global security, disarmament, health, and protection of the environment and of natural resources for the present and future generations. The extension of the G8 to other regions certainly constitutes important and significant progress; yet at the time of the negotiations and concrete and operational decisions, it is necessary to take into careful consideration all needs, not only those of the countries that are most important or that have a more marked financial success. In fact, only this can make these decisions actually applicable and sustainable over time. Let the voices of Africa and of the less economically developed countries be heard! Let effective models be sought in order to link the decisions of the various groups of countries, including the G8, with the United Nations Assembly. In this way each nation, whatever its political and financial importance, may legitimately express itself in a position of equality with the others.

Lastly, I would like to add that the decision of the Italian government to host the G8 in the city of L'Aquila, a decision approved and shared by the other member states and guests, is particularly significant. We have all witnessed the generous solidarity of the Italian people and of other nations, of national and international organizations toward the populations of the Abruzzo region hit by the earthquake. This mobilization of solidarity could constitute an invitation to the members of the G8 and to the governments and peoples of the world to face united the current challenges that place humanity with no possibility of postponement before crucial decisions for the destiny of mankind itself, which is closely connected with the destiny of creation.

❧

## More Agricultural Investments in Poor Countries

From Message to Mr. Jacques Diouf, Director General
of FAO, on the Occasion of World Food Day 2009,
October 16, 2009

If the celebration of World Food Day recalls the foundation of the FAO and its action in the fight against hunger and malnutrition in the world, it stresses above all the urgent need for interventions on behalf of all who are without daily bread, in so many countries, because of inadequate food security.

The actual crisis that is hitting all sectors of the economy without distinction is particularly harshly affecting the world of farming, whose situation is becoming dramatic. This crisis demands that governments and the different elements of the international community make decisive and effective decisions.

To guarantee people and peoples the possibility of overcoming the scourge of hunger is to assure them concrete access to adequate, healthy food. Indeed, this is a practical expression of the right to life which, although it is solemnly proclaimed, all too often remains far from being implemented fully.

The theme chosen by the FAO for World Food Day is: "Achieving Food Security in Times of Crisis." It is an invitation to consider agricultural work as a fundamental element of food security and consequently as fully part of economic activity. For this reason, farming must have access to adequate investments and resources. This topic calls into question and makes clear that by their nature the goods of creation are limited: they therefore require responsible attitudes capable of encouraging the sought-after security, thinking likewise of that of future generations. Thus profound solidarity and farsighted brotherhood are essential.

The realization of these objectives entails a necessary change in lifestyle and mindsets. It obliges the international community and its institutions to intervene in a more appropriate and forceful way. I hope that such an intervention may encourage cooperation with a view to protecting the methods of cultivating the land proper to each region and to avoiding a heedless use of natural resources. I also hope that this cooperation will preserve the values proper to the rural world and the fundamental rights of those who work the land. By setting aside privileges, profit, and convenience, it will then be possible to achieve these objectives for the benefit of the men, women, children, families, and communities that live in the poorest regions of the planet and are the most vulnerable. Experience shows that even advanced technical solutions lack efficiency if they do not put the person first and foremost, who comes first and who, in his or her spiritual and physical dimensions, is the alpha and the omega of all activity.

Rather than an elementary need, access to food is a fundamental right of people and peoples. It will therefore become a reality, hence a security, if adequate development is guaranteed in all the different regions. The drama of hunger in particular can only be overcome by "eliminating the structural causes that give rise to it and promoting the agricultural development of the poorer countries. This can be done by investing in rural infrastructures, irrigation systems, transport, organization of markets, and in the development and dissemination of appropriate agricultural technology that can make the best use of the human, natural, and socio-economic resources that are more readily available at the local level."[49]

Faithful to her vocation to be close to the most deprived, the Catholic Church promotes, sustains, and participates in the efforts made to enable each people and each community to have access to the necessary means to guarantee an appropriate level of food security.

## For Development to Be Sustainable It Is Necessary to Aim at a Balance between Farming, Industry, and Services

From Angelus, November 14, 2010

In the Second Reading of today's liturgy, the Apostle Paul underlines the importance of work for the life of man. We are reminded of this idea on Thanksgiving Day, which is traditionally celebrated in Italy on this second Sunday in November, as the offering of thanks to God at the end of the harvest season. Although in other geographical areas farming periods naturally differ, today I would like to draw inspiration from St. Paul's words to reflect on agricultural work in particular.

The full gravity of the current economic crisis, discussed

---

49. Benedict XVI, *Caritas in Veritate*, n. 27.

these past few days at the G20 summit, should be understood. This crisis has numerous causes and is a strong reminder of the need for a profound revision of the model of global economic development.[50]

It is an acute symptom which has been added to a long list of many far more serious and well-known problems, such as the lasting imbalance between wealth and poverty, the scandal of world hunger, the ecological emergency, and the now widespread problem of unemployment.

In this context, a strategic revitalization of agriculture is crucial. Indeed, the process of industrialization has often overshadowed the agricultural sector, which although benefiting in its turn from modern technology has nevertheless lost importance with notable consequences, even at the cultural level. It seems to me that it is time to re-evaluate agriculture, not in a nostalgic sense but as an indispensable resource for the future.

In the present economic situation, the dynamic economies are tempted to pursue advantageous alliances, which nevertheless may have detrimental results for other poorer states, situations of extreme poverty among the masses and the depletion of the natural resources of the earth that God has entrusted to man, as it says in Genesis, so that he may till it and keep it.[51] And in spite of the crisis it can still be seen that in the old industrialized countries, lifestyles marked by unsustainable consumerism are encouraged. These also prove damaging for the environment and for the poor. Then a really concerted aim for a new balance between farming, industry, and services is necessary so

50. Cf. Benedict XVI, *Caritas in Veritate*, n. 21.
51. Cf. ibid.

that development may be sustainable, so that no one will lack bread and work, air and water, and that the other fundamental resources may be preserved as universal rights.[52] Thus it is essential to cultivate and spread a clear ethical awareness that is equal to facing the most complicated challenges of our time. Everyone should be taught to consume in a wiser and more responsible way. We should promote personal responsibility along with a social dimension of rural activities based on the undying values of hospitality, solidarity, and sharing the toil of labor. Many young people have already chosen this path and many professionals are also returning to agricultural enterprises, feeling that in this way they are not only responding to personal and family needs but also to a *sign of the times,* to a concrete sensibility for the *common good.*

Let us pray to the Virgin Mary that these reflections may serve as an incentive to the international community, as we thank God for the fruits of the earth and the work of mankind.

## The Farmer as a Model of a Mentality That Unites Faith and Reason

From Angelus, December 12, 2012

Advent calls us to develop inner tenacity, resistance of the spirit, which enables us not to despair while waiting for a good that is slow in coming, but on the contrary to prepare for its coming with active trust.

52. Cf. ibid., n. 27.

"Behold," James writes, "the farmer waits for the precious fruit of the earth, being patient over it until it receives the early and the late rain. You also be patient. Establish your hearts, for the coming of the Lord is at hand" (Jas 5:7–8).

The comparison drawn with the farmer is very expressive; he has sown the field and has before him several months of patient and constant waiting, but he knows that in the meantime the seed completes its cycle, thanks to the autumn and spring rains. The farmer is not a fatalist but the model of a mentality which unites faith and reason in a balanced way. For on the one hand he knows the laws of nature and does his work well, and on the other, he trusts in Providence, because certain fundamental things are not in his hands but in the hands of God. Patience and constancy are truly a synthesis between human commitment and confidence in God.

## Adequate Food Concerns the Fundamental Right to Life

From Address to Participants in the
Thirty-seventh Conference of FAO,
July 1, 2011

1. I am particularly glad to welcome you who are attending the thirty-seventh conference of the Food and Agriculture Organization of the United Nations. You are perpetuating a long and happy tradition, inaugurated sixty years ago at the time the FAO was established in Rome.

Mr. President, through you I would like to thank the many

government delegations that have wished to be present at this meeting, thereby witnessing to the effective universality of the FAO. I would also like to renew the Holy See's support for the organization's praiseworthy and indispensable work and to confirm that the Catholic Church is committed to collaborating with your endeavor to respond to the real needs of numerous brothers and sisters in humanity.

I take this opportunity to greet Mr. Jacques Diouf, the director general who, with competence and devotion, has enabled the FAO to face the problems and crises brought about by the changing global situations which are affecting, even dramatically, its specific field of action.

I extend my most sincere good wishes to Mr. José Graziano da Silva, recently elected director general, for the success of his future activity, while I express the hope that the FAO may respond increasingly and ever better to the expectations of the member states and contribute practical solutions for people suffering from hunger and malnutrition.

2. Your work has identified the policies and strategies that can contribute to the important revitalizing of the agricultural sector, the level of food production, and the more general development of rural areas. The present crisis that is now affecting all aspects of the economic and social situation requires, in fact, that no effort be spared to eradicate poverty, the first step to save millions of men, women, and children from starvation who have no daily bread.

However, a complete reflection requires a search into the causes of this situation that is not limited to levels of production, to the increasing demand for food, or the fluctuation of prices: factors which, although important, risk causing the drama to be read exclusively in technical terms.

Poverty, underdevelopment, and consequently hunger are often caused by selfish attitudes which, read in the human heart, emerge in the social activity of human beings, in their arising trade, in market conditions, and in the lack of access to food, resulting in the denial of the primary right of every person to be nourished, hence free of hunger.

How can we gloss over the fact that food itself has become an object of speculation or indeed is linked to the development of a financial market which, with no set rules and practically no moral principles, seems attached to the single goal of profit?

Adequate food concerns the fundamental right to life. To guarantee it also means intervening directly on those factors in the agricultural sector which negatively affect productivity on the mechanisms of distribution and on the international market. And all this when a global food production, according to FAO and authorized experts, is able to feed the world population.

3. The international framework and frequent anxiety engendered by instability and rising prices demands practical and necessarily unitary responses in order to obtain better results that states cannot guarantee individually. This means making solidarity an essential criterion for every political action and every strategy, so as to make international activity and its legislation as many instruments of effective service to the human family in its entirety, and, in particular, to the neediest people.

It is therefore urgently necessary to have a developmental model which does not only consider the economic importance of needs or the technical viability of the strategies to be pursued, but also the human dimension of all initiatives. It must also be capable of achieving authentic brotherhood,[53] relying on the ethical recommendation of "giving food to the hungry" which is part of the sentiment of compassion and humanity engraved in every person's heart and which the Church numbers among the works of mercy.

In this perspective, the institutions of the international community are called to work consistently, following their mandate in order to support the values proper to human dignity by eliminating closed attitudes and without leaving room for private concerns to be passed off as in the general interest.

4. The FAO is also called to renew its structure, throwing off the obstacles that hinder the realization of the purpose stated in its constitution: raising levels of nutrition, securing improvements in the efficiency of the production and distribution of all food and agricultural products, and bettering the condition of rural populations so as to free humanity from hunger.[54]

To this end, full harmony of the organization and governments becomes essential in order to guide and support projects, especially in the present situation when available economic and financial resources are diminishing, while the number of hungry people in the world is not falling in accordance with the hoped-for goals.

5. I am thinking of the situation of millions of children who, as the principal victims of this tragedy, are condemned to a premature death and to a delay in their physical and psychological

53. Cf. ibid., n. 20.
54. Cf. Constitution of the Food and Agriculture Organization of the United Nations, Preamble.

growth or who are forced into forms of exploitation to receive even a minimal quantity of food.

Attention to the young generations can be a way of countering the abandonment of rural zones and farm work, to permit entire communities whose survival is threatened by hunger to envisage their future with greater confidence.

We are, in fact, obliged to note that, in spite of the commitments made and the consequent obligations, help and concrete aid is frequently limited to emergencies, forgetting that a consistent conception of development must be able to outline a future for every person, family, and community, favoring long-term goals.

Thus the chosen projects must also be supported by the international community as a whole, in order to rediscover the value of the rural family business and to support its central role in order to achieve stable food security. Indeed, in the rural world the traditional family nucleus is endeavoring to promote agricultural production through the wise transmission by parents to their children not only of systems of cultivation or of the preservation and distribution of food, but also of lifestyles, principles of education, culture, the religious sense, and the conception of the sacredness of the person in all the stages of his or her existence. The rural family is not only a work model, but a model of living and a concrete expression of solidarity, in which the essential role of women is confirmed.

Mr. President, ladies and gentlemen,

6. The aim of food security is an authentically human requirement, as we are aware. To guarantee it to the present generations and to those that are to come also means protecting natural re-

sources from frenzied exploitation, since the consumer race and consequent waste appear to pay no attention at all to the genetic patrimony and biological differences that are so important for agricultural activities. Moreover, the idea of an exclusive appropriation of these resources is opposed to the call that God addresses to men and women, so that by tilling the earth and preserving it (cf. Gn 2:8–17) they may encourage participation in the use of the goods of creation, an aim that international multilateral activity and legislation can certainly contribute to achieve.

In our era when, in addition to the numerous problems that besiege agricultural work there are new opportunities to contribute to resolving the drama of famine, you can strive to ensure that by guaranteeing the food that corresponds to their needs, each and every one may develop in accordance with their true dimension as creatures made in the likeness of God.

This is the wish I would like to express as I invoke upon you and upon your work an abundance of divine blessings.

## *Agricultural Work as an Objective Strategy of Growth and Integral Development*

From Message to Mr. Jacques Diouf, Director General of FAO,
on the Occasion of World Food Day 2011, October 17, 2011

1. While the annual celebration of World Food Day wishes to commemorate the foundation of the FAO and its commitment to agricultural development to combat hunger and malnutrition, it is also an opportunity to emphasize the plight of so many of our brothers and sisters who lack daily bread.

The painful images of the numerous victims of hunger in the Horn of Africa impress us, as every day another chapter is added to what is one of the worst humanitarian catastrophes in recent decades. Immediate aid is of course essential in the face of the death from starvation of entire communities obliged to abandon the land of their origins, but it is also necessary to intervene in the medium and long term so that international intervention is not limited to responding only to emergencies.

The situation is increasingly complicated by the difficult crisis that is affecting different sectors of the economy worldwide and is hitting the most deprived, besides affecting agricultural production and the consequent possibility of access to foodstuffs. Nevertheless, the effort of the governments and of the other members of the international community must be oriented to efficient coordination, aware that liberation from the yoke of hunger is the first concrete expression of the right to life which, in spite of being solemnly proclaimed, is often very far from being effectively put into practice.

2. The theme chosen for this day, "Food Prices: From Crisis to Stability," rightly invites us to reflect on the importance of the different factors that can provide individuals and the community with essential resources, starting with farming that must not be seen as a secondary activity but as the focus of every strategy of growth and integral development. This is even more important if we take into account that the availability of food is increasingly conditioned by the fluctuation of prices and sudden climate changes. At the same time we are seeing a steady abandonment of rural areas with a global decrease in agricultural production and therefore of food reserves. In addition, it seems,

unfortunately, that here and there the idea of considering food-stuffs as any commercial product is spreading and therefore also subjected to speculation.

The fact cannot be glossed over that despite the progress achieved to date and the promise of an economy that increasingly respects every person's dignity, the future of the human family needs a new impetus if it is to overcome the current fragile and uncertain situation. Although we are living in a global dimension there are evident signs of the deep division between those who lack daily sustenance and those who have huge resources at their disposal, who frequently do not use them for nutritional purposes or even destroy reserves. This confirms that globalization makes us feel closer but does not establish fraternity.[55] This is why it is necessary to rediscover those values engraved on the heart of every person that have always inspired their action: the sentiment of compassion and of humanity for others, the duty of solidarity, and the commitment to justice must return to being the basis of all action, including what is done by the international community.

3. In the face of the widespread drama of hunger, the invitation to reflection, the analysis of problems, and even the readiness to intervene are not enough. All too often these factors remain unexpressed, because they pertain to the emotional sphere and fail to jog the conscience and its quest for truth and goodness. There are frequent intentions to justify the conduct and omissions dictated by selfishness and by vested interests. On the contrary this day aims to be a commitment to modify

---

55. Cf. Benedict XVI, *Caritas in Veritate*, n. 19.

forms of conduct and decisions that ensure, today rather than tomorrow, that every person has access to the necessary food resources and that the farming sector has a sufficient level of investments and resources that are able to stabilize production, and hence the market. It is easy to reduce any consideration of the need for food to the growth of a population, knowing well that the causes of hunger have other roots and that they have taken a heavy toll on life among many a poor Lazarus who is not allowed to sit at table with the rich Epulo.[56]

In fact it is a question of adopting an inner attitude of responsibility, able to inspire a different lifestyle, with the necessary modest behavior and consumption, in order thereby to promote: the good of future generations in sustainable terms; the safeguard of the goods of creation; the distribution of resources; and above all, the concrete commitment to the development of entire peoples and nations. On their part, the beneficiaries of international cooperation are conscientiously to employ solidarity funds "by investing in rural infrastructures, irrigation systems, transport, organization of markets, and in the development and dissemination of agricultural technology that can make the best use of the human, natural, and socio-economic resources that are more readily available at the local level."[57]

4. It will be possible to put all this into practice if the international institutions also guarantee their service with impartiality and efficiency, but fully respecting the deepest convictions of the human spirit and every person's aspirations. In this perspective the FAO can contribute to guaranteeing adequate nutrition

56. Cf. Paul VI, *Populorum Progressio*, n. 47.
57. Benedict XVI, *Caritas in Veritate*, n. 27.

for all, to improving the methods of cultivation and of trade and to protecting the fundamental rights of those who work the land, without forgetting the most authentic values which the rural world and those who live in it preserve.

The Catholic Church feels close to the institutions that are committed to guaranteeing food. Through her structures and development agencies, she will continue to accompany them actively in this effort to ensure that every people and community has the necessary food security and that no compromise or negotiations, however authoritative, can guarantee, without real solidarity and authentic brotherhood. "The importance of this goal is such as to demand our openness to understand it in depth and to mobilize ourselves at the level of the 'heart,' so as to ensure that current economic and social processes evolve toward fully human outcomes."[58]

With these sentiments, Mr. Director General, I hope that you will pursue your commitment to the neediest people which has characterized these years of responsibility and dedication, while I invoke abundant blessings of the Almighty upon the FAO, upon each one of the member states, and upon the whole staff.

58. Ibid., n. 20.

# SCRIPTURAL INDEX

# GENERAL INDEX

ACEA (Municipal Electricity and Water Board), 118–20
Adam and Eve, 42
Advent, 87, 199
Afghanistan, 55
Africa, 54–55, 134–35, 168, 191–92, 194, 206
Agnelo, Geraldo Majella Cardinal, 11
agriculture, 142–44, 153–55, 166; deterioration of, 41, 186; respectful of environment, 47–48, 55; revitalization of, 159, 174–76, 178, 195–99, 201–8
AIDS, 163–64
alternative energy, 106, 111–12, 124–25, 183–84
Amazon, 10–12
Angola, 54
Armenia, 59
Apostles, 24, 28, 31–32, 173
Apostolic See. *See* Holy See
Aquinas, Thomas, 54
Argentina, 59
atmosphere, xiii, 30, 72
Augustine, 126

Båge, Lennart, 174
Baptism, 5, 24–25, 27, 65
Bartholomew I (Ecumenical Patriarch), 10–13
Basil of Caesarea, xii
Benedict XV, 102
Benedict XVI, ix–x, xii–xiv, xvii; *Caritas in Veritate,* xiv–xvi, 33, 39, 50, 53, 119, 191; *Deus Caritas Est,* 95–96; *Introdu-*

*tion to the Spirit of the Liturgy,* xii; *Spe Salvi,* 107
Berlusconi, Silvio, 189
biocentrism. *See* ecocentrism
biosphere, xiii
Brazil, 11
Bükk, ix

Cambodia, 59
Cameroon, 54
capitalism, 150
Carmelites, 101
charity, 35, 37, 46, 48–49, 95–97, 101, 173, 190–91
Chernobyl, 94
Chile, 59
Christianity: activity, 12, 127; communities, 60, 94, 173; historical nature of, xi; identity, xiv–xv, 25, 58, 63, 69, 93–94, 97, 99, 128, 142, 146, 173; and ideology, x; manifold nature of, xi, 11
Chrysostomos II (Archbishop of Nea Justiniana and all Cyprus), 18
Church, xvii, 4, 27, 31–33, 49–53, 66–67, 70–71, 81, 85, 98, 110, 123, 187, 190, 192, 209; as Body of Christ, 28; social teaching, 95–96, 134, 142, 153, 156, 160, 167, 172–73, 175–77, 180, 197, 201, 20
climate change, 19–20, 41, 47, 97–98, 157–59, 190, 206
Columban, 58
Columbia, 59
common good, 46, 48, 75–76, 95, 100,

common good *(cont.)*
103–4, 119–20, 135, 140, 142, 146–48, 158, 167–69, 199
consumerism, xvi–xvii, 24, 47–48, 111, 156, 179, 186, 198, 204–5
Creation. *See* ecology; humanity; nature
Curia, 101

Darfur, 56
deforestation, 22, 41
democracy, 57, 192
Democratic Republic of the Congo, 56
demographics, 145, 162–63
Descartes, xi
desertification, 8, 22, 41, 54–55, 135, 186
Diouf, Jacques, 139, 150, 153, 157, 195, 201
discrimination, 58, 107, 114–15
disease, 18, 40, 112–13, 163–64. *See also* AIDS
drugs, 23, 55

Easter, 65–67, 69, 78
ecocentrism, 51
ecology: and consequences of human disregard for, 20, 22, 33–34, 38–39, 85, 107, 135, 183; economy, xiii, 19–20, 36, 41, 44, 73, 98, 124–25, 134–35, 150, 186; and education, 48, 57, 64–65, 86, 111, 117, 187–88, 192; and ethics, xiii, 40, 50, 71, 110; human, 14–15, 19, 33, 36, 49–50, 61, 73, 86, 120, 132, 162, 187; and human responsibility, ix, 20–21, 33–34, 39, 43, 46, 48–51, 54, 62, 67, 71, 73, 86, 100–101, 104, 117, 133; of nature, 19, 33, 36, 61, 100–101, 131–32, 187; and peace, 14–16, 26 38–60, 116–17, 186–87; and power, xv; social, 14, 23–24, 26. *See also* nature
Ecuador, 59
ecumenism, 57–58, 108; Catholic and Orthodox, 12, 18

education, 75, 143, 155, 164, 204
Egypt, 60; ancient, 78–79, 81
electricity, ix
Elizabeth, St., 29
emissions, ix
Enlightenment, 128–29
environment. *See* ecology; nature
environmental degradation, xvi, 32, 40–44, 47–48, 50, 53, 56, 109–11. *See also* ecology; pollution
erosion. *See* desertification
Etchegaray, Roger Cardinal, 10
Eucharist, 7–8, 27–28, 70, 82–83, 149. *See also* Jesus Christ
eugenics, 114–15
European Union, 57–58, 145–47
evolution, 39, 68, 86, 182
Exodus, 77–80

family, 3, 26, 47–50, 65, 75, 86, 94, 104–6, 143, 155, 159, 164, 188, 193, 204; of humanity, xvi, 17, 19, 22, 40, 44–45, 60, 96, 100, 135, 141, 157, 161, 166, 172, 185, 202, 207
famine, 110, 139, 205. *See also* hunger
Feast of the Visitation, 29
Flygenring, Elín, 111
Food and Agriculture Organization (FAO), 139–42, 150–51, 153, 157–58, 160, 195–96, 200–203, 205, 208–9; World Summit on Food Security, 54
food supply, 54, 100, 140, 143, 155, 157–59, 174–75, 177–78, 197, 201–6; right to, 41, 150–53, 179, 196; speculation, 124, 206–7. *See also* hunger
Fourth Symposium on the Adriatic Sea, 11
Francis of Assisi, xii, 5, 14, 35, 84–85, 87
Franciscan, xii, xiv–xv, 83–85

G8, 189–95
G20, 197–98

Galileo Galilei, 91

Gandhi, Mohandas, 16

garden: as image, xiv, 4–5

genetically modified organisms, xiii

German Basic Law, 128–29

Germany, xii, 126–28, 131

Glendon, Mary Ann, 95

globalization, 74, 161, 166–68, 170–73, 207

God, 15; as Creator, xiv–xv, 4–6, 9, 12–13, 22–23, 26, 34, 39–40, 42, 51, 67, 71, 84–86, 132–33; entrusting nature to man, ix, xiv–xv, 13, 36, 73, 85, 121; intervention in history, xi, 7, 9; as Love, 6, 68, 93–94, 188; as Reason, 68, 93–94, 123. *See also* ecology; humanity; Holy Spirit; Jesus Christ; Kingdom of God; Word of God

Gospel, 7, 26–27, 36–37, 62, 95, 97, 99, 107, 148, 156. *See also* Scripture

Graziano da Silva, José, 201

Greenland, 20

Guinea, 60

Hafnarfjordur, 101

Haydn, Joseph, 29

Heraclitus of Ephesus, xv, 43n30, 182n36

holidays, 3. *See also* tourism

Holy Land. *See* Jerusalem

Holy See, 36, 57, 59, 100–102, 111, 125, 157, 160, 174, 190–91, 201

Holy Spirit, 24–32; as Creator, 4–6; gifts of, 27

Honduras, 60

humanity, as created in image of God, xiv, 13, 22, 26, 31, 42, 58, 121, 147, 153; and culture, xv, 15, 41–42, 50, 108, 120–21, 130–33, 162, 175, 183; development of, 14–15, 33–35, 38–41, 47–49, 63–64, 86, 96, 98, 101, 112, 116, 120, 171, 188–89, 205; dignity of, 14, 20, 26, 51, 53, 61, 75, 96, 99, 115, 126–27, 133, 140–41, 147, 155–56, 158, 204, 207; digni-

ty of unborn, 54, 163, 187; and duties toward creation, xiv, xvi, 11, 18–19, 42, 64, 73, 185; and freedom, 24, 53, 58, 60–61, 68, 93, 104, 106, 132, 140; and labor, 8; nature of, 15–16; as part of Creation, 39, 42, 64, 67, 182; primacy of, x–xi, 42–43, 51, 73–75, 96, 113–14, 182–83; relation to God, 20, 64, 67, 200; and rights, xiv, 16–17, 20, 26, 41, 133, 147, 152, 179, 199; and soul, 10

hunger, 18, 35, 106, 110, 139, 142–44, 150–60, 166, 169, 174–78, 195–98, 201–8. *See also* famine; food supply

Iceland, 99–101, 111–12

Ilulissat Icefjord, 20

industry, xiii, 14, 20–21, 48, 55, 166, 172, 198–99

International Atomic Energy Agency (IAEA), 102

international community, 45, 47, 55, 58–60, 72–74, 97–98, 100–101, 103–4, 106–7, 111–12, 158, 160, 165, 208; co-operation, 105, 145, 169, 171, 174–75, 185–86, 190, 196, 206; levels of development, 105–6, 168, 174–75, 184, 189; trade, 167–70, 179–81

International Fund for Agricultural Development (IFAD), 174–75

Iran, 60

Iraq, 60

Israel, 59–60; ancient, 66, 69, 78–81

Italy, 59, 84, 190, 197

James, 200

Jerusalem, 59–60

Jesus Christ, 6–8, 24–28, 30–31, 37, 52, 61, 66, 83, 96, 107, 117–18, 121, 149, 177–78; and Eucharist, 7–8; and *Logos,* 124; and Passion, 9–10, 71, 77; Resurrection, 32, 38, 65, 70–71. *See also* God; Word of God

*The Garden of God: Toward a Human Ecology*
was designed in Dante by Kachergis Book Design of Pittsboro,
North Carolina. It was printed on 60-pound Natures Natural
and bound by Thomson-Shore of Dexter, Michigan.